MARK TWAIN

MARK TWAIN

A WRITER'S LIFE

BY MILTON MELTZER

Franklin Watts
New York • London • Toronto
Sydney • 1985

Illustrations from the Author's Collection

Library of Congress Cataloging in Publication Data

Meltzer, Milton, 1915–
Mark Twain: a writer's life.

Bibliography: p.
Includes index.
Summary: Surveys the life of Samuel Clemens, who
grew up in Missouri, was a river pilot on the
Mississippi, became a journalist, and achieved
fame as a writer under the pen name Mark Twain.
1. Twain, Mark, 1835–1910—Biography—Juvenile
literature.   2. Authors, American—19th century—
Biography—Juvenile literature. [1. Twain, Mark,
1835–1910.   2. Authors, American] I. Title.
PS1331.M37   1985   818'.409 [B] [92]   85-5108
ISBN 0-531-10072-3

CONTENTS

MARK TWAIN

For Jessica, Ira, and David

1

THAT HALF-FORGOTTEN PARADISE

It wasn't his real name, of course. Samuel Langhorne Clemens was what they christened him. He was born on the 30th of November, 1835, in the almost invisible village of Florida, Missouri. West of the village lay Indian territory, just 200 miles off. A hundred people lived in Florida, and Mark increased the population by one percent. It was more than many of the best people in history could have done for a town, he said. The village had two streets, a few lanes, rail fences, and cornfields all around. You walked in deep dust in dry times, through black mud in wet. Most of the houses were of logs, but a few were frame. Mark's birthplace was a two-room clapboard house, rented.

He was a seven-month child, a feeble baby who barely made it through that winter and the next year. "When I first saw him," said his mother, "I could see no promise in him. But I felt it was my duty to do the best I could. He was a poor looking object to raise." Long after, when Jane was in her eighties, Mark asked her if she wasn't uneasy about him in his infancy. "Yes, the whole time," she said. "Afraid I wouldn't live?" A long pause. "No, afraid you would."

Mark's parents, John and Jane Clemens, both came from small slaveholding families, always scrabbling for a living. They were of mixed English and Irish stock, and took pride in their pre-Revolutionary War heritage.

Their families settled in Virginia and then spread into the Kentucky frontier. Among Mark's ancestors were members of the Quaker faith, a persecuted sect in those times. That heritage of a Quaker conscience may have had something to do with Mark Twain's leaning toward pacifism, his resistance to authority, his instinctive sympathy for underdogs and minorities, and his hatred for cruelty in any form.

John Clemens was an ambitious, hard-working man, always haunted by the specter of poverty. A stepchild, he had to support himself by the age of fourteen. There was no time for play or fun in his boyhood, nor did he get much affection. He apprenticed to a lawyer and earned a license to practice law in Kentucky. A tall lean man with piercing gray eyes, he was known for a hot temper and a grim mouth that never laughed.

John married Jane Lampton, a pretty woman with thick red hair, slow Southern speech, and a love for dancing. Her charm and wit made her an unlikely mate for cold and stern John. In his boyhood Mark noticed that his mother and father were always kind to each other, but nothing warmer. His mother's natural affection was chilled by his father's reserve.

Law practice on the frontier was too poor to support a growing family. So John Clemens tried farming or storekeeping, shifting from place to place as both his health and his fortunes crumbled. Deciding to try their luck on the far side of the Mississippi River, John and Jane moved to the tiny hamlet of Florida, where Mark, their fifth child, was born.

After failing to make a go of it in Florida, John Clemens picked up again, moving the family to Hannibal, thirty miles away. There he opened a general store on Main Street. No one could make a fortune in that sleepy little river town. But out of the fourteen youthful years he spent in that "half-forgotten Paradise," Mark Twain was to draw the memories from which he shaped *Tom Sawyer* and *Huckleberry Finn* and *Life on the Mississippi*.

The Mississippi River's vast variety—its woods, the birds on its sandbars and islands, the villages along its shores, the keelboats and barges and broadhorns and flatboats and steamboats that moved up and down its muddy waters, and the human democracy they carried—all went into the making of a writer. Many years later, roaming the world, Mark Twain found no one, he said, whom he had not met before on the river.

Mark started school when he turned five. Missouri had no public schools in those early days. He went to a private school in a small log house. Mrs. Horr, the teacher, charged twenty-five cents per week per pupil. She opened school with a prayer and a reading from the Bible. Taking as the text, "Ask, and ye shall receive," she said you only had to pray hard and sincerely enough to get what you wanted. Mark gave this fresh idea a trial and prayed for gingerbread. The baker's daughter brought a slab of gingerbread to school every day and tried to keep it out of sight. But when Mark finished his prayer that morning, there it was in easy reach—and the girl not looking. "In all my life I never enjoyed an answer to a prayer more than I enjoyed that one," he said.

Good manners, spelling, and reading were the staples of the school. For those who wanted more, Hannibal offered a library, a few magazines and newspapers, roving lecturers, and home-made political oratory. Mark was not an eager pupil. If he won any prizes for learning, they have not been found. The most important things he learned were not picked up at school.

Every boy in that village on the west bank of the Mississippi had one ambition—to be a steamboatman. Once a day a packet

*Twain's hometown on the Mississippi—Hannibal,
Missouri. The drawing was made by the artist
Henry Lewis around 1846, when Mark was a boy.*

boat arrived upward from St. Louis, and another down from Keokuk. Not only the boys but the whole village looked forward to those arrivals at the stone-paved wharf. When a drayman with a quick eye spotted a film of dark smoke in the sky, he would shout "S-t-e-a-m-b-o-a-t a-comin'!" and in a twinkle sleepy Hannibal was alive and moving. Everyone hurried down to the wharf to watch the coming boat as though it were a wonder they were seeing for the first time. And she was a handsome sight, as Mark Twain painted it:

> She is long and sharp and trim and pretty; she has two tall, fancy-topped chimneys, with a gilded device of some kind swung between them; a fanciful pilot-house, all glass and gingerbread, perched on top of the texas deck behind them; the paddleboxes are gorgeous with a picture or with gilded rays above the boat's name; the boiler deck, the hurricane deck, and the texas deck are fenced and ornamented with clean white railings; there is a flag gallantly flying from the jack staff; the furnace doors are open and the fires glaring bravely; the upper decks are black with passengers; the captain stands by the big bell, calm, imposing, the envy of all; great volumes of the blackest smoke are rolling and tumbling out of the chimneys—a husbanded grandeur created with a bit of pitch pine just before arriving at a town; the crew are grouped in the forecastle; the broad stage is run far out over the port bow, and an envied deck-hand stands picturesquely on the end of it with a coil of rope in his hand; the pent steam is screaming through the gauge-cocks; the captain lifts his hand, a bell rings, the wheels stop; then they turn back, churning the water to foam, and the steamer is at rest.
>
> Then such a scramble as there is to get aboard, and to

get ashore, and to take in freight and to discharge freight,
all at once and the same time; and such a yelling and
cursing as the mates facilitate it all with! Ten minutes
later the steamer is under way again, with no flag on the
jack staff and no black smoke issuing from the chimneys.
After ten more minutes the town is dead again, and the
town drunkard asleep by the skids once more.

Boy after boy managed to work on the river—as engineer, fireman, clerk, pilot. Pilot was the greatest position of all. A princely salary, and no board to pay. It was Mark's grandest ambition. He dreamed that someday he would run away and not come home until he was a pilot and could come in glory.

Mark was born only some fifty years after the American Revolution. The United States had a long way to go before it would reach the Pacific Coast. With only twenty-four states, its population numbered fifteen million. (Metropolitan New York alone has more than half that many people now.) It was an adolescent nation, with little interest in foreign affairs. All eyes were on expansion westward.

Two million Americans were black slaves, denied any right of citizenship. That slavery could continue to flourish in a nation founded on the belief that all people are created free and equal was a cancer in the body politic. But the vast majority of Americans accepted it. Only a tiny band of abolitionists dared oppose it.

The best-seller of Mark's childhood was *The Young Christian,* a book bought by parents to stuff every boy and girl full of piety. James Fenimore Cooper's *Leatherstocking Tales* of the Indian frontier were enormously popular. So were Longfellow's poems and Dana's *Two Years Before the Mast.* Schoolmarms

urged their pupils to read the *Peter Parley* books. Mass-produced
by hack writers, these preachy juveniles sold in the millions.

Mark wouldn't be caught dead with *Peter Parley*. He learned
much better stories from the lips of black folk like his father's
slave-of-all-work, Ned. His horrifying story of the man who lost
his Golden Arm no child could ever forget. Mark learned to tell
tall tales from the community of slaves who lived in the cabins
on the small farms of Missouri—stories about the terrors of the
night, of evil spells and the dead that walked, of death lurking
at every bend of road or river.

The Clemens children saw with their own eyes what slavery
was. They remembered a runaway slave captured by six white
men who tied him up with ropes and left him groaning on the
floor of a deserted shack. Mark never forgot the time when Jenny,
the house slave, was threatened with a whip by Jane Clemens
for "uppity" behavior. Jenny snatched away the whip but paid
for her courage when John Clemens rushed in, bound her wrists,
and lashed her with a bridle rein.

Once Mark saw a dozen black men and women chained to
one another, lying on the pavement, awaiting shipment to a slave
market in the Deep South. Theirs were the saddest faces he ever
saw. Another time, he remembered, a white man killed a black
man for some trifling offense, and everybody was indifferent. They
only felt sorry for the slave's owner, who had lost a valuable
property.

Nights young Mark went on coon or possum hunts with the
blacks, making long marches through the gloom of woods, tin-
gling when the distant bay of a dog announced the game was
treed. Then the wild scramblings and stumblings through briers
and bushes and over roots to get to the spot, the lighting of a
fire and the felling of the tree, the joyful frenzy of the dogs, the
weird picture it made in the red glare—and the delight everyone

got out of it, except the coon. In the chill, gray dawns there were wild pigeon hunts and squirrel hunts and prairie chicken hunts and wild turkey hunts. When the sun rose it poured light and comfort all around, and everything was fresh and dewy and fragrant, and coming home just in time for breakfast, Mark knew life was a blessing.

"Never smoke more than one cigar at a time" was Mark's sole rule of abstinence when he grew up. But earlier, at fourteen, he had had a brief spasm of interest in the Hannibal chapter of the Cadets of Temperance. From colonial times people had joined groups to reform drunkards and eliminate liquor. The cadets didn't allow a boy to smoke or drink or swear. Mark, like most children, couldn't resist becoming a member of something or other. And he didn't care shucks what it was, either. Didn't they wear beautiful red scarves and walk in solemn procession when a distinguished citizen died? He stood it for all of three months, then sidled out. "I liked the red scarfs well enough," he said, "but I could not stand the morality."

Nor could he take his mother's constant dosing of her sickly boy with balms, bitters, and balsams. She subscribed to all the health periodicals and believed the solemn ignorance they were inflated with. He couldn't stand their rules as she applied them to him—when to go to bed, when to get up, what to eat and drink, how much exercise to take, what frame of mind to keep oneself in, what sort of clothing to wear. "It was all gospel to her," he complained, and he the handy victim of the quackery.

Being dosed with Osgood's India Chocologue or Rogers' Liverwort and Tar was no fun. But he could forget his sorrow when the circus or the minstrel shows came to town. Right there in Hannibal he saw CHANG AND ENG, THE WORLD RENOWNED SIAMESE TWINS, and HOMIO AND IOLA, THE WILD AUSTRALIAN CHILDREN. And there was Dan Rice's Hippodrome, boasting over 200 men and horses. Dan's stupendous establishment offered the gaping boys and girls the Bedouins of the Desert, Feats of the Gymnasium, Olympic Sports, Acrobatics and Terpsichore, all accompanied by a Double Brass Band led by the Wizard Bugler. Adults—50 cents; Children—half-price.

Even more excitement touched Hannibal when news of gold found at Sutter's Mill infected many villagers with California yellow fever. Bankrupt Ben Horr, husband of Mark's first schoolteacher, headed west and so did Mark's playmate, John Robards, whose father captained a company of gold hunters.

When Mark was eleven his father died. John Clemens was caught in a sleet storm, chilled to the bone, and developed pneumonia. No medicine of that day could help, and his gaunt body gave in. Aware he was on his deathbed, he drew his daughter Pamela to him, kissed her (for the first time, Mark said), and gave the death rattle. One of Mark's most shocking memories of childhood came next. Through a keyhole he watched the family doctor take advantage of an available corpse to dissect his father's wasted body. That night and for several nights running, Mark walked about the house in his sleep with a sheet wrapped around him. It horrified his mother, who never forgot it.

It was even harder going for the family after John Clemens's death. Mark's older brother Orion, working as a printer in St. Louis, sent some of his pay, and Pamela's fees from piano pupils helped too. Mark could no longer loaf after school; he had to find work. He became a delivery boy for the local paper.

He looked his age—eleven—and his sickly days were long gone. Now his body was tanned and tough. His head, too large for his small size, was covered with sandy curls he tried to slick down with water. He had blue-green eyes, a firm jaw, an aquiline nose, and a mouth quick to grin. Already he had that soft, lazy drawl picked up from his Southern mother. It gave his voice a charming turn that would delight audiences when he took to the lecture platform.

With his father gone, Mark drew closer to his mother, now the head of the household. A slim little woman, she had aged under the burden of poverty and seven children. Quick to speak her mind, she would thwack Mark on the head with her thimble when he got out of line. But she was gentle and generous, "always the heart of a young girl," Mark said. She liked to play cards, loved the theater, and was fond of jokes and playful duels of wit. Mark captured some of her qualities when he drew upon her for Aunt Polly in *Tom Sawyer*.

When a weekly newspaper moved to Hannibal in 1848, Mark was taken on as an apprentice. "Printer's devil," they called it. No wages, but room and board and a suit of clothes. The suit was a hand-me-down that fitted like a circus tent. The "room" was a mattress thrown on the floor of the print shop. The board was so pitiful that he and the other two apprentices stole potatoes and onions from the boss's cellar and cooked them secretly on the office stove.

Mark began as the *Courier*'s drudge, doing all the dull and dirty work, from starting the fire on winter mornings to bringing water from the town pump to picking up the scattered type on the floor and sorting the good from the broken. Thursdays at dawn he delivered the freshly printed sheets around town, dodging nips from the short-tempered dogs.

He learned to become a capable and swift journeyman printer. His bright mind and readiness to learn something new moved him up to subeditor. He liked the smell of printer's ink. "There is something in the very atmosphere of a printing office, calculated to awake the mind and inspire a thirst for knowledge," wrote a country editor of that time. As it had been for Ben Franklin, the print shop became the "poor boy's college" for Mark Twain.

In 1850 Mark's brother Orion left St. Louis and came back to Hannibal to start a new weekly paper he called the *Western*

*Jane Clemens, Mark's mother, painted by
an itinerant artist in St. Louis*

Mark Twain at 15 as an
apprentice printer. Note
"SAM" on his belt buckle.

Union. Soon after, Mark quit his no-pay apprenticeship on the *Courier* and joined his brother's paper. For some two years he served Orion as printer and editorial assistant. Orion was twenty-five now, but Mark, fifteen, would not play the role of submissive younger brother. Nor was Orion capable of enforcing discipline upon Mark. Orion was an honest, gentle, absent-minded man who detested printing and business; he might have been happier as a country preacher. He worshiped Ben Franklin, but could never apply his rules for success to his own life.

When Orion hired Mark he promised him $3.50 a week, a wage the boy never collected. At least Mark could sleep again under his mother's roof, though the food wasn't much better. And he enjoyed working alongside his younger brother Henry, newly apprenticed to Orion.

A few days after Orion took Mark on, a fire broke out at 1 A.M. in a grocery next door to the print shop. It became the occasion for Mark's first venture into print. His humorous report on the fire appeared in the *Western Union* on January 16, 1851. Mark was fifteen.

The *Western Union* did badly. Orion was a poor businessman. Few people paid for their subscriptions or their advertisements. In place of cash they dumped on the office floor cordwood, cabbages, turnips, parsley, cotton rags. But was the paper worth any more? Mark said later that like most village newspapers it was "a wretchedly printed little sheet, being very vague and pale in spots, and in other spots so caked with ink as to be hardly decipherable." It was stuffed with local ads run again and again just to fill space long after their paid lifetime had expired. The columns were littered with glorified quack medicines, tired fiction, sappy poetry, and alleged "wit and humor." There was very little local news, even though Hannibal, now swollen to 2,500, must have had something worth noting. But

then, this was before editors thought to send out reporters to actually find the news.

To the Wit and Humor column Mark obviously contributed his own unsigned scribblings. There are patches of writing showing a lively playfulness, including a funny piece about
the first bloomer costume seen in Hannibal. In the spring of 1852,
Mark tried for recognition as a writer beyond the borders of
Hannibal. He mailed a sketch to a comic weekly in Boston, the
Carpet-Bag. It was about a show-off trying to impress ladies on
a steamboat and getting his comeuppance. Published on May 1,
it was signed by his initials, S.L.C. It was much like the home-
spun humor found in most papers of the time.

When Orion left town for a week, Mark took over as editor
and sprinkled the pages with tales of hoaxes and with "villain-
ous" illustrations carved on the wooden type by his jackknife.
Like many humorous writers of that day, he adopted a pen name,
choosing W. Epaminondas Adrastus Blab.

Numerous fires enlivened Hannibal, one of them damaging
Orion's shop so badly he had to move the press into his mother's home. Another fire destroyed the village jail, killing a drun-
ken tramp confined there for the night. Mark was ridden with
guilt, for just before the tramp was picked up he had given the
man some matches for his pipe. The tramp, smoking on the straw
cot, had set fire to the jail, and with the keys lost, the battering
ram broke down the door too late. Mark and the townsfolk
shuddered outside as the pitiful cries of the tramp died away.
The horror of death by fire haunted his imagination, and would
be worked into his stories.

Hannibal in the early 1850s was what one critic has called
"a nest of singing birds." By that he meant poets whose ambition soared far above their talent. Publishers floated cargoes of
gift books and annuals leaking sentimental and sickly poetry.
Mark, too, had a go at it. In his brother's absence he printed

"Love Concealed," eighteen lines of verse signed by "Rambler" and dedicated to "Miss Katie of H———L." He thought it excruciatingly funny to abbreviate Hannibal so that it could be confused with Hell. More exuberant clowning appeared under Mark's new pen name, including a mock defense of all redheads, with the conjecture that Adam and Jesus Christ must have had hair the color of his own.

After nearly three years as Orion's helper, Mark was ready to break free of home. Hard work had given him enough self-confidence, going on eighteen, to try his luck in the world. He was excited by reports of the Crystal Palace Fair in New York: twenty thousand people coming every day to see the spectacle! Why not himself? But that might scare his mother. So he told her only that he would go to St. Louis, where his sister Pamela and her husband lived, and find work there. He promised his mother he would not drink or gamble while he was gone and, with his scanty belongings, left Hannibal for good.

2

PILOT ON
THE
MISSISSIPPI

In June he took the night boat to St. Louis, visited his sister, and found a job in the composing room of a newspaper. He stayed just long enough to earn the money for the trip to New York. He had never traveled on a railroad before. It took five jolting days and nights to go from St. Louis to Chicago to Buffalo to Albany, and then by Hudson River steamboat down to New York. He wrote home about the trip, and Orion published his letter proudly on September 8, 1853—the first of many travel letters by Twain that would delight the public.

Of course he went straight to America's first World's Fair at the Crystal Palace on Fifth Avenue and 42nd Street. (It was near the spot where the Public Library stands today.) Then he started work at a print shop, earning four dollars a week. After he paid for his board and laundry, he had about fifty cents to salt away. With nobody at home to talk to, he spent his evenings reading happily at a free printer's library with an amazing collection of 4,000 books; had anyone ever seen more books in one place? For a boy who had detested school it was quite a change. He kept writing home that he would quit New York any day now, but he found to his amazement that he liked the "abominable place" and put off leaving. Besides, there was his beloved theater to attend: What night in Hannibal could compare with seeing the great actor Edwin Forrest play the role of Spartacus, leader of the Roman slave revolt?

Still, he hungered for a sight of more big cities, and went down to Philadelphia where he found nightwork subbing as a typesetter on the *Inquirer*. After a morning's sleep he would visit historic sites, art galleries, and libraries, educating himself. He liked this city better than New York. At eighteen he felt himself a man, no longer a boy, yet homesickness could make him miserable. When winter came on he traveled to Washington to see the capital's sights.

A straggling town then, the capital did not impress Mark. The few public buildings were grand, but seemed out of place amid the cluster of poor brick houses that looked as though they had been emptied out of some giant's sack and scattered abroad by the winds. He visited the Senate chamber to gawk at the men who gave the people the benefit of their wisdom and learning for a little glory and eight dollars a day. Again he saw Edwin Forrest, this time as Othello, and thought the National Theater the only thing of consequence in Washington.

Unaccountably, he drifted back to New York to work for a while and, in the summer of 1854, finally went back West. He sat up three days and nights in the train to reach St. Louis. He spent a few hours with Pamela, then took the boat to Muscatine, Iowa, where the family had moved when Orion bought the local paper. He surprised them at breakfast, and they embraced joyfully after a separation of fifteen months.

Orion urged Mark to join the paper, but Mark felt he couldn't afford to work for nothing. He went back to his old job on the St. Louis *Evening News*, rooming with a young chairmaker named Frank Burroughs, who introduced him to the novels of Dickens, Scott, and Thackeray. They became close friends. Some twenty years later the two exchanged impressions of one another in that youthful time. Mark wrote:

> *As you describe me I can picture myself as I was 22 years ago. The portrait is correct. You think I have grown some; upon my word there was room for it. You have described a callow fool, a self-sufficient ass, a mere human tumble-bug, stern in air, heaving at his bit of dung, imagining that he is remodeling the world and is entirely capable of doing it right. . . . That is what I was at 19–20.*

In the summer of 1855 Mark joined Orion again. His brother had married and moved to Keokuk, Iowa. With his younger brother Henry, now seventeen, Mark worked in Orion's Ben Franklin Book and Job Printing Office. The pay was five dollars a week and board. Mark and Henry slept in the office.

Mark joined a singing class, perhaps because there were many girls in it. He played piano and guitar passably, and he had a good singing voice. His openness and sense of fun made him popular, but though he was twenty, his interest in girls seemed to stop at the friendship stage. They noticed that he always had a book with him—a Dickens novel, the tales of Poe, or a history.

Nothing eventful happened in Keokuk except for his debut as an after-dinner speaker. His hilarious speech at a printers' banquet so impressed the audience that he was promptly recruited into a debating society. They cared less about his logic than about the laughter.

Orion still had no system of work and no gift for making money. The business was so shaky he found it hard to pay Mark's wages, so he took him into partnership and paid him nothing at all. But Mark in those days cared little for money. If he could manage to eat and had a place to sleep, it was enough. His mother had moved to Pamela's house and was well cared for.

Suddenly he was seized with Amazon fever. A pair of Americans had made a survey of the upper Amazon, and their report on the exploration of the great river was being widely read. Mark got hold of it and promptly decided he would head for South America, harvest the coca plant, and make a fortune. His impulse overruled any thought of ways and means. Fifty years later he recalled that moment and what it revealed of his nature:

> *In all that time my temperament has not changed by even a shade. I have been punished many and many a time, and bitterly, for doing things and reflecting afterward, but these tortures have been of no value to me; I still do the thing commanded by Circumstance and Temperament, and reflect afterward. Always violently. When I am reflecting on these occasions, even deaf persons can hear me think.*

He didn't have a dime to finance the grand expedition. But one bleak and windy day, walking down Main Street, he saw a bit of paper fly by him and lodge in a wall nearby. He reached for it absently and discovered it was a fifty dollar bill—a denomination he was a total stranger to. His conscience induced him reluctantly to advertise his finding, but no one claimed it. So he used it to head for Cincinnati on the first leg of a journey to the Amazon. He took a printing job in Cincinnati to tide him over the winter of 1856.

In his cheap boardinghouse he made a friend of a lanky Scotsman double his age and with not a fraction of his humor. But the dour Macfarlane had a powerful intellect and shelves of serious books. Nights they talked till ten, when the Scot grilled a herring and the conversation ended. Macfarlane was one of those rare people who can change a young person's life. He was a walking encyclopedia, a living dictionary, and a true thinker. Before Darwin had published his theory of evolution, the Scot was thinking in the same direction. But he drew an unhappy conclusion: Evolution had produced humankind but stopped too soon. Man had not developed morally. He was the only creature in the animal kingdom capable of malice and vindictiveness. His mental powers were superior, but they were used only to keep other beasts in servitude and captivity, along with millions of his own kind. Later in life Mark's own writings would echo Macfarlane.

With winter in Cincinnati coming to an end, Mark began dreaming again about coca hunting in the Amazon. In April 1857 he boarded the *Paul Jones*, bound for New Orleans, from where he could sail for South America. As it steamed slowly down the Ohio, the "permanent ambition" of boyhood reawakened. His Hannibal schoolmates, the Bowen boys, all three of them, had become pilots; maybe he could too.

Horace Bixby was at the wheel of the *Paul Jones*. He thought cub pilots were more trouble than they were worth. But for three days Mark laid siege to him. The young fellow with the great tangle of red hair amused Bixby and he let him take the wheel for a while. Finally he said he'd teach him the river for $500, and board free. Mark had nothing like that sum. He figured he could borrow $100 from Pamela's husband without straining his credit. How about $100 cash and the rest when I earn it? he asked. Bixby was taken with this young man. Not just his slow pleasant speech, his relaxed manner with the wheel, his sincere purpose, but something underneath. His intelligence? His warmth? He accepted Mark's terms, and they began as teacher and pupil at once. By the time they reached New Orleans, Mark had almost forgotten he'd been a printer, and the Amazon had faded away.

In *Life on the Mississippi,* a book Mark wrote a quarter of a century later, he recalled how he learned the 1,200 miles of the great changing, shifting river with the easy confidence of young ignorance. If he had really known what it would demand of his wits, he would not have had the courage to start. He had supposed all a pilot had to do was keep his boat in the river. How much of a task could that be, with the river so wide?

He was a good pupil, with a natural taste for the river and a fine memory. But what an appalling task he had taken on! He had to get the entire river by heart, to know it like the ABC. Bixby made him squirrel away in a notebook everything he told him. In *Life on the Mississippi,* Mark pokes fun at himself, giving us this description of one of Bixby's piloting lessons:

One day he turned on me suddenly with this settler:

"What is the shape of Walnut Bend?"

He might as well have asked me my grandmother's opinion of protoplasm. I reflected respectfully, and then said I didn't know it had any particular shape. My gun-powdery chief went off with a bang, of course, and then went on loading and firing until he was out of adjectives . . . I waited. By and by he said:

"My boy, you've got to know the shape of the river perfectly. It is all there is left to steer by on a very dark night. Everything else is blotted out and gone. But mind you, it hasn't the same shape in the night that it has in the daytime."

"How on earth am I ever going to learn it, then?"

"How do you follow a hall at home in the dark? Because you know the shape of it. You can't see it."

"Do you mean to say that I've got to know all the million trifling variations of shape in the banks of this interminable river as well as I know the shape of the front hall at home?"

"On my honor, you've got to know them better than any man ever did know the shapes of the halls in his own house."

*The ambitious cub pilot besieging Captain
Horace Bixby to teach him the river in a
sketch from Twain's* Life on the Mississippi

"I wish I was dead!"

"Now, I don't want to discourage you, but—"

"Well, pile it on me; I might as well have it now as another time."

"You see, this has got to be learned; there isn't any getting around it. A clear starlight night throws such heavy shadows that, if you didn't know the shape of a shore perfectly, you would claw away from every bunch of timber, because you would take the black shadow of it for a solid cape; and, you see, you would be getting scared to death every fifteen minutes by the watch. You would be fifty yards from shore all the time when you ought to be within fifty feet of it. You can't see a snag in one of those shadows, but you know exactly where it is, and the shape of the river tells you when you are coming to it. Then there's your pitch-dark night; the river is a very different shape on a pitch-dark night from what it is on a starlight night. All shores seem to be straight lines, then, and mighty dim ones, too; and you'd run them for straight lines, only you know better. You boldly drive your boat right into what seems to be a solid, straight wall (you know very well that in reality there is a curve there), and that wall falls back and makes way for you. Then there's your gray mist. You take a night when there's one of these grisly, drizzly, gray mists, and then there isn't any particular shape to a shore. A gray mist would tangle the head of the oldest man that ever lived. Well, then, different kinds of moonlight change the shape of the river in different ways. You see—"

"Oh, don't say any more, please! Have I got to learn the shape of the river according to all these five hundred thousand different ways? If I tried to carry all that cargo in my head it would make me stoop-shouldered."

"No; you only learn the shape of the river; and you learn it with such absolute certainty that you can always steer by the shape

that's in your head, and never mind the one that's before your eyes."

"Very well, I'll try it; but, after I have learned it, can I depend on it? Will it keep the same form, and not go fooling around?"

Before Mr. Bixby could answer, Mr. W. came in to take the watch, and he said:

"Bixby, you'll have to look out for President's Island, and all that country clear away up above the Old Hen and Chickens. The banks are caving and the shape of the shores changing like everything. Why, you wouldn't know the point about 40. You can go up inside the old sycamore snag now."

So that question was answered. Here were leagues of shore changing shape. My spirits were down in the mud again. Two things seemed pretty apparent to me. One was that in order to be a pilot a man had got to learn more than any one man ought to be allowed to know; and the other was that he must learn it all over again in a different way every twenty-four hours. . . .

I went to work now to learn the shape of the river; and of all the eluding and ungraspable objects that ever I tried to get mind or hands on, that was the chief. I would fasten my eyes upon a sharp, wooded point that projected far into the river some miles ahead of me and go to laboriously photographing its shape upon my brain; and just as I was beginning to succeed to my satisfaction we would draw up to it, and the exasperating thing would begin to melt away and fold back into the bank! . . .

It was plain that I had got to learn the shape of the river in all the different ways that could be thought of—upside down, wrong end first, inside out, fore-and-aft, and "thort-ships,"—and then know what to do on gray nights when it hadn't any shape at all. So I set about it. In the course of time I began to get the best of this knotty lesson, and my self-complacency moved to the

*front once more. Mr. Bixby was all fixed and ready to start it to
the rear again. He opened on me after this fashion:*

*"How much water did we have in the middle crossing at Hole-
in-the-Wall, trip before last?"*

I considered this an outrage. I said:

*"Every trip down and up the leadsmen are singing through
that tangled place for three-quarters of an hour on a stretch. How
do you reckon I can remember such a mess as that?"*

*"My boy, you've got to remember it. You've got to remember
the exact spot and the exact marks the boat lay in when we had
the shoalest water, in every one of the five hundred shoal places
between St. Louis and New Orleans; and you mustn't get the
shoal soundings and marks of one trip mixed up with the shoal
soundings and marks of another, either, for they're not often twice
alike. You must keep them separate."*

When I came to myself again, I said:

*"When I get so that I can do that, I'll be able to raise the
dead, and then I won't have to pilot a steamboat to make a living. I want to retire from this business. I want a slush-bucket
and a brush; I'm only fit for a roustabout. I haven't got brains
enough to be a pilot; and if I had I wouldn't have strength enough
to carry them around, unless I went on crutches."*

*"Now drop that! When I say I'll learn a man the river I mean
it. And you can depend on it, I'll learn him or kill him."*

The river was another—and a huge—chapter in Mark's educa-
tion. In the streets of Hannibal, in the print shops of several cities, he had learned something about human nature. The river
deepened and broadened his understanding of the vast variety of
American life. In those four years of schooling, he said, he got
to know all the different types of human nature to be found in
fiction, biography, or history. He loved the profession of piloting far better than any other he followed after, he said, and took

a measureless pride in it. Kings, presidents, clergymen, even writers, are manacled servants of the public, he claimed. Everybody has a master and frets in servitude. But the Mississippi pilot in his time had none. He was absolute monarch when at the wheel.

Bixby was not always his teacher, for sometimes the river trade took him away. Then Mark would be assigned to other pilots, one of them so mean and tyrannical Mark would go to bed and dream of killing him in seventeen different ways—all of them new.

When he had been on the river a year, he was rated a fine steersman. Still, as an apprentice, he was getting no wages. A steamboat made a round trip in thirty-five days, with a day or two of idle time at either end. Mark snatched the time in New Orleans to work nights on the levee guarding freight. The few dollars earned he spent to replace worn-out clothing. On the long night watches he imagined "all sorts of situations and possibilities," and they got into many a chapter he wrote later on.

At the St. Louis end of the run Mark stayed with Pamela's family. Once, visiting aboard a boat at the dock, he met Laura, a fifteen-year-old girl he fell hard for. When her boat left in a few days he wrote to her, but she never replied. He did not see her again until forty-eight years later, when both were married, widowed, and old, and he learned she had never received his letter.

When Mark was working on the packet *Pennsylvania* as cub pilot, he got his brother Henry, now twenty, a job as clerk. The pilot, an arrogant man, got into a dispute with Henry and struck him in the face. Enraged, Mark knocked the pilot down. The captain offered Mark the pilot's job, but he didn't feel up to the responsibility after only one year on the river. He left the boat at New Orleans, with Henry staying on. Four days later the boilers of the *Pennsylvania* blew up, killing 150 people, including Henry.

*A portrait of Mark Twain painted
about 1859 when he earned his certificate
as a Mississippi River pilot*

Mark always blamed himself for his brother's death. His face, friends noticed, took on the serious, pathetic look it would always have in repose. His vitality did not diminish nor did his temperament change. But at twenty-three, he looked thirty; at thirty, nearer forty.

That September Mark won his license as Mississippi River pilot, and Bixby made him his full partner. After an apprenticeship of eighteen months he was master of a much-admired profession and earned the same income as the vice president of the United States. With plenty of money in his pocket, he helped his mother and Orion generously. His childhood ambition had been achieved by the age of twenty-three. His popularity and his glory were great. In the hangouts of the pilots he spun yarns so funny he convulsed his listeners, all the while keeping a poker face.

There is evidence that Mark wrote only a little while piloting on the river. In the election of 1860 Abraham Lincoln won the presidency on a platform calling for restricting the spread of slavery. The Southern states began rushing out of the Union. Lincoln took office on March 4, and six weeks later Fort Sumter was fired upon.

The Civil War had begun.

3

ADVENTURES IN THE WEST

There was hot talk in the pilots' club of what to do about the war. Some said they would go with the Union, others with the Confederacy. Horace Bixby chose the North's side. Mark couldn't make up his mind. He wanted to go home and think about it. He sailed upriver as a passenger. Along the way he saw soldiers drilling on the shore and military supplies piling up. Nearing St. Louis, a cannon shell exploded in the river right in front of the boat, and they halted abruptly. Theirs was the last steamboat allowed to make the trip from New Orleans to St. Louis. Mark didn't know it then, but his pilot days were over.

From St. Louis he went to Hannibal to see old friends. He found that several military units were forming in and about the town, with mixed and confused aims. They wanted to defend their patch of Missouri from invaders—but which?

Mark joined a company of a dozen young fellows, mostly schoolmates pledged to go with Missouri. A border slave state, its allegiance was bitterly fought for by North and South. (It finally voted to stay in the Union.) Mark's men had no uniforms and only what equipment they scrounged at home. Neighbors pitched in with worn-out horses and mules that transformed them into a cavalry. Mark's mount was a small yellow mule with tail trimmed in a tassel. His equipment was a pair of gray blankets, a homemade quilt, a frying pan, a carpetbag, a small valise, an overcoat, twenty yards of rope, an umbrella, and an ancient Kentucky rifle.

They pitched camp on the Salt River, making a log stable their headquarters. With a pair of sheepshears they trimmed their hair in what they hoped was a dashing military style, and then they elected their officers. So many titles were handed out that only three privates were left to fill the ranks. Mark was voted second lieutenant.

No one relished guard duty; when Mark was stuck with it he fell asleep in the hot sun. One day he developed a painful boil and sought horizontal comfort in hay piled in a horse trough, all the while cursing war and the fools who invented it.

Running out of food, the company foraged on the farms nearby. One angry woman drove them away with a hickory pole when she learned they were Confederates: Her husband was a Union colonel. They bedded down one night in a hayloft, and Mark awoke scorched by flames. One of the boys had fallen asleep smoking. Mark leaped from the loft and sprained his ankle, multiplying the misery of his boil. The disaster swelled his disgust with army life, the Confederacy, and the human race. His ankle was so painful he had to stay in bed for a few weeks to recover.

When he was able to move about again, it was to get as far as he could from the war. (Later, in an essay, he explained he had "resigned" from the Confederate Army after two weeks' service because he was "incapacitated by fatigue through persistent retreating.") His devotion to the Southern cause evaporated quickly. He slipped away to Keokuk to talk with Orion, an abolitionist and a staunch Union supporter.

Mark came at just the right moment. An old friend of Orion's had risen high in the Lincoln administration, and Orion had been made secretary of the new territory of Nevada, second in rank only to its governor.

Mark envied his brother. He wrote: "I coveted his distinction and especially the long strange journey he was going to make, and the curious new world he was going to explore. . . . Pretty soon he would be hundreds and hundreds of miles away on the great plains and deserts, and among the mountains of the Far West, and would see buffaloes and Indians, and prairie dogs, and antelopes, and have all kinds of adventures, and maybe get hanged or scalped, and have ever such a fine time."

But the always-broke Orion lacked the funds to reach his new post. Mark had the solution: They would both go, and Mark would dip into his pilot savings to pay for their overland passage to Nevada.

They packed at once, said good-bye to the family in St. Louis, and took the boat for St. Joseph, where they caught the overland stage in late July 1861. For nineteen days and nights, covering 1,700 miles behind sixteen galloping horses, never stopping but for meals or to change teams, they headed into the sunset.

In mid-August the dusty brothers climbed down from the stage in Carson City, Nevada; population: 2,000. In those first few months of exploring his corner of the frontier, Mark learned that "the country is fabulously rich in gold, silver, copper, lead, coal, iron, quicksilver, marble, granite, chalk, plaster of Paris (gypsum), thieves, murderers, desperadoes, ladies, children, lawyers, Christians, Indians, Chinamen, Spaniards, gamblers, sharpers, coyotes, poets, preachers, and jackass rabbits . . . It never rains here, and the dew never falls. No flowers grow here, and no green thing gladdens the eye. The birds that fly over the land carry their provisions with them."

After the sagebrush and alkali deserts of Nevada,
San Francisco was paradise to Mark Twain.
He dressed up fancy and danced with the girls
in a step peculiar to himself—and the kangaroo.

His pieces were horseplay humor, frontier stuff, for which he got no pay. As July and Mark's resources came to an end, the *Enterprise* offered him twenty-five dollars a week to turn reporter. It's also possible that he was hired so that the *Enterprise* would get government printing contracts from his brother Orion, the territorial official.

On a hot September day the ex-printer, ex-pilot, ex-soldier, ex-miner dropped into the *Enterprise* office and announced, "My name is Clemens, and I've come to write for the paper." He had hiked the 130 miles to Virginia City to make a new beginning that would, this time, see him through to a dazzling end.

4

REPORTER
AT
LARGE

Mark turned to newspaper work with only a little amateur experience behind him. For a young man he was remarkably cocksure. And so was the entire staff of the *Enterprise*—all, like Mark, still in their twenties. The paper's duty was "to keep the universe thoroughly posted concerning murders and street fights, and balls and theaters, and packtrains, and churches, and lectures, and city military affairs, and highway robberies, and Bible societies, and by-wagons, and the thousand other things which it is in the province of local reporters to keep track of and magnify into undue importance for the instruction of the readers of a great daily newspaper."

The young bachelors who put out the paper were "full to the brim with the wine of life." The office was like a fraternity house where every man could do what he liked and there was no one to say no. Mark wrote local news—often seasoned by his extravagant humor—an occasional unsigned editorial, letters sent from Carson City, San Francisco, or wherever he happened to be, and reports of sessions of the territorial legislature. Much of his writing was gossipy and whimsical, anticipating the humorous columnists who would be so popular in the twentieth century. Frontier journalism was casual and careless; the writers easily slipped free of facts to veer into fantasy or satire.

But Mark also produced a good deal of solid and responsible reporting. For part of his apprenticeship was the writing of daily dispatches from the legislature's sessions in Carson City. He teamed with a man skilled in shorthand reporting, and the two combined to turn out some 4,000 words a day. Besides their *Enterprise* salaries they were paid a bonus of seven dollars a day by the legislature. Their reports became the official record.

It was while he was on the *Enterprise* that Mark began to use the pen name Mark Twain. Pseudonyms for writers were quite common in that time. They signified an invented personality, a mask. When readers saw that name they looked for a unique perspective upon people and events, and usually a comic one. But for his routine political reporting Mark still signed himself Samuel L. Clemens. It was the personal journalism, mostly humorous, that he signed Mark Twain. He fished up that name from his piloting days on the Mississippi. Later he said that name had been used by Captain Isaiah Sellers, a retired pilot who wrote pieces for a New Orleans paper. But there is no evidence that Sellers ever used that name. Anyhow, it was a good pen name, brief, crisp, unforgettable. It was an old river term, of course, a leadsman's call, signifying two fathoms, or twelve feet, which meant safe water.

The *Enterprise*, only two years old when Mark joined it, had boomed into a great daily, printed by steam press. It had five editors and twenty-three compositors, and was housed in its own brick building. There was a competing daily, the *Union*, and the reporters on both papers loved to indulge in mock duels in print. The columns were sprinkled with scurrilous abuse, hoaxes, jibes, put-downs. When victims were not at hand, Mark would kid himself in print. Such comedy was popular, but it was rarely good enough to foreshadow the major writer Twain would be-

Eds. Golden Era: — Going down to San José last Sunday, to write a letter to the newspaper with which I am connected, I was taken somewhat sick, & the "Unreliable" being along, I ventured to entrust him with my work. I send you the result, for I have no use for it myself. This is the twentieth time I have been deceived by that well-meaning but ~~unstable~~ unstable young man, & it shall be the last. Every time he gets a commission of this kind, he calls himself an editor, & gets drunk — to prove it, perhaps, though I cannot conceive how he hopes to establish such a fact by such an argument.

Yours, sadly,

Mark Twain.

This is perhaps the earliest "Mark Twain" signature known. He wrote this letter to the Golden Era editors when he and his friend, C. T. Rice, whom he dubbed the "Unreliable," were visiting San Francisco in September 1863.

come. He made several close friends and felt top of the heap. No wonder he could write to his mother and sister that "I am proud to say I am the most conceited ass in the Territory."

Perhaps he was encouraged in his conceit by the approval he won from one of the country's best-loved humorists, Artemus Ward (a pen name, too—his real name was Charles F. Browne). Ward came to Virginia City for a few days to deliver his platform talks to crowded audiences. But he stayed on three weeks because he found Mark and his newspaper pals such delightful company. Nightly, on a rising tide of humor, Mark showed off his wit at the dinner table, and earned Ward's applause. Maybe he too could win fame and honor? Their companions agreed Mark was Ward's equal in intelligence and originality. With Ward urging him on, Mark sent a piece to the New York *Sunday Mercury*, which published it early in 1864. He had made his first mark as a writer in the big time.

More proof of his powers came when Mark was invited to deliver the "governor's address" to a burlesque of the territorial legislature right after its closing session. It was Mark's first public opportunity as a lecturer. What he planned was not truly a lecture at all, but a theatrical monologue. The place was packed, and he let himself go. He ridiculed the governor, the legislators, and the most prominent citizens of the capital. From his first drawling sentences the audience was in a storm of laughter and applause. At the end they gave him a gold watch inscribed to "Governor Mark Twain." It looked as though a new platform star had been born.

But he did more than provoke laughter and cover the doings of the legislators. At least a few times he crusaded against injustice. He attacked undertakers who extorted gross profits from mourning families and prosecuting attorneys who could not tell their own witnesses from those of the defense.

Despite all the freedom and variety of his work during the

boom years of the Humboldt mines, he began to show signs of wanting something different. Was he tired of staying in one place so long (hardly two years)? Did he want to go somewhere special? No, he didn't know what he wanted. But he had spring fever, and needed a change.

At the end of May 1864, he took the stagecoach for San Francisco. He did not yet know the imaginative power hidden within him. Yes, he was a writer, and a pretty good one, and he had proved himself as a professional journalist. But that the experiences of his twenty-eight years on earth would one day provide the materials for his major books—of this he had no idea.

In San Francisco Mark found a job on the *Daily Morning Call*. But the routine of the *Call* was a disappointment to a veteran of the free and easy *Enterprise*. Crimes, horse races, street squabbles, fires: "It was fearful drudgery—soulless drudgery—and almost destitute of interest. It was an awful slavery for a lazy man." But the town's literary circle provided relief, and their publications offered new markets for the now-professional writer.

Although he found his work dull, he discovered San Francisco to be "a truly fascinating city to live in, stately and handsome at a fair distance, but close at hand one notes that the architecture is mostly old-fashioned, many streets are made up of decaying, smokegrimed, wooden houses, and the brown sandhills towards the outskirts obtrude themselves too prominently."

He took life easy. The *Call* paid him twenty-five dollars a week and agreed to give him no night work. He got up at ten and quit work at five or six. "I work as I always did, by fits and starts," he wrote home. He added to his readership and his income by writing pieces for two literary papers, the *Golden Era* and the *Californian*.

The *Call* was still his daily bread, but when it would not print his attacks on the corruption of local politicians and police he sent the dispatches to his old paper, the *Enterprise*. He was

The wandering reporter, photographed not long
after his arrival in San Francisco

revolted by the brutal treatment of the Chinese in San Francisco, and damned the mobs that hunted victims in the streets. The Chinese had come to dig in the goldfields and build the railroads. It was their labor that pioneered the West's farmlands and fisheries, but race prejudice denied them jobs and justice. Instead, they got low wages, abuse, and violence. Although Mark denounced the violence, like most writers of his time he succumbed to the stereotypes, and without meaning to do harm, wrote comedy that ridiculed the immigrants.

The literary weeklies were the center of the city's Bohemian group. In their offices Mark ran into the poet Joaquin Miller, the actress Ada Isaacs Menken, the rising young literary star Bret Harte, and the humorists Artemus Ward and Orpheus C. Kerr. They clustered here behind the Sierras, which the transcontinental railroad would not cross for some years.

A number of Mark's humorous sketches appeared in the weeklies during 1864–65. He decided he could survive without the *Call* and quit just as they were about to fire him. He arranged to send a daily letter to the *Enterprise*, reporting on San Francisco in his own way, getting thirty dollars a week for this work.

Naturally, he went on attacking the city's rank corruption, but so ferociously that the police chief sued the *Enterprise* for libel. Letting the police cool off, Mark visited his friend Jim Gillis, a miner, in his cabin on Jackass Hill in the Tuolumne district. Gillis was a superb storyteller who handed on to Mark some of his most delightful tales. (Dick Baker's cat in *Roughing It*, the jaybird and the acorns in *A Tramp Abroad*, and the Royal Nonesuch in *Huckleberry Finn*.)

In those dreary winter months, Mark tried his hand again at mining in the California gold mine region. In the notebook he began to keep in January 1865 the most frequent jottings are "rain," "beans," "dishwater." But on one page is the entry:

"Coleman with his jumping frog—bet a stranger $50.—stranger had no frog and C. got him one:—In the meantime stranger filled C's frog full of shot and he couldn't jump. The Stranger's frog won." The story, an old one, Mark first heard from Ben Coon, a marathon talker mining at Angel's Camp. Late in February Mark got back to San Francisco and found a letter from Artemus Ward asking for a sketch for Ward's new book. But Ward's book had gone to press. So Mark wrote the frog story and sent it to a New York paper instead. Called "Jim Smiley and His Jumping Frog," it was carried in the New York *Saturday Press* for November 18, 1865. He had learned that the "humorous story depends for its effect upon the manner of its telling." Papers copied it everywhere. The whole country laughed. It was the beginning of Mark's fiction writing, the foundation of a towering fame. But to Jane and Pamela, Mark complained that people had singled out "a villainous backwoods sketch" to compliment him on.

A month after Mark was back in San Francisco, the Civil War—and slavery—ended. But the bloody convulsion was not reflected in the potboilers he lived on now. He wrote casual sketches for the West Coast papers, finding fun even in his first earthquake, which shook the city in October.

"Jim Smiley's Frog," trifling though he thought it, gave him added prestige for having been published in the East. He grew restless again, and when he learned that a new steamship was sailing for the Sandwich Islands (as Hawaii was then called), he saw it as a chance to do something different. He induced the Sacramento *Union* to send him to report on life in the islands. A veteran of domestic newsletters, he was now a foreign correspondent. It would be the first sea voyage for the ex-river pilot. And it would be his first chance to do sustained writing. He boarded the *Ajax* in March 1866 and eleven days later arrived in Honolulu. With his fame preceding him, he was warmly welcomed.

He had meant to "ransack the islands" for a month. The month stretched out to five. His travel letters began in the *Union* in April, and were promptly popular. Sometimes they even made page one. Mark was absorbed in new people and places, and his fresh responses came through in his travel pieces. "No careworn or eager, anxious faces in this land of happy contentment," he wrote in his notebook. "God, what a contrast with California and Washoe!"

He sent the *Union* about twenty-five letters describing the great volcanoes, cataracts, and mountains, the Kanaka royalty, the broad plantations, and the few friends from Nevada who had strayed this far west. He seasoned the bouillabaisse with the anecdote, satire, and burlesque that characterize all his travel writing. Hawaii, he wrote home, "has been a perfect jubilee to me in the way of pleasure."

Late in June Mark returned to Honolulu from a tour of all the islands. He was worn out, and forced to bed down with saddle boils. He wanted only rest and quiet, but a startling event disrupted his plans. On that very day, June 21, 1866, an open boat with fifteen seamen washed up on a Hawaiian beach. For forty-three days, with only ten days' provisions, the men had been smashed about on a stormy sea. Their clipper ship, the *Hornet*, had taken fire with a cargo of kerosene aboard and burned to the line. Mark saw his chance for a great story if he could interview the castaways and get a dispatch aboard a ship sailing for San Francisco the next morning. He had himself carried on a cot to the Honolulu hospital. While an American diplomat questioned the survivors, Mark took notes. Then he stayed awake through the night to write the story of the struggle to survive six weeks of drifting across 4,000 miles of open sea. In the morning, just as the ship cast off for California, Mark's story was tossed aboard.

His account of the *Hornet* disaster was carried safely to the States, and on July 1 the *Union* spread it across four columns of the front page. Mark had produced a spectacular newspaper scoop, one of the biggest in history. The suffering of the *Hornet* crew, and their heroism, created a sensation and added to Mark's fame. On the day the story was published he sailed from Hawaii—never to return—and twenty-five days later was back in San Francisco. Awaiting him was a $300 bonus for the scoop.

"Home again," he wrote in his notebook. "No—not home again—in prison again, and all the wild sense of freedom gone. The city seems so cramped and so dreary with toil and care and business anxiety. God help me, I wish I were at sea again!"

That restlessness was a dominant trait in his personality (some say, in the *American* personality). Tiring quickly of staying in one place, he was always moving around. Was he chasing adventure? Or was he trying to find in change itself the solidity he couldn't find in permanence?

When the blues seized him, he could shake them off only if he got to work again. He prepared an article on the *Hornet* disaster and sent it to *Harper's Magazine*. To his delight the editors accepted it. Maybe he could do a series on Hawaii, and turn it into a book and some royalties? And what about a trip around the world, reporting as he went? But first, he'd take advantage of the popularity of his Hawaii letters and deliver a lecture on that subject.

It would be his first lecture for money. Nervously, he arranged to take the new opera house at half rates. He wrote a burlesque of the typical show business advertisement, announcing "the Trouble to Begin at 8." At a dollar a head, 1,800 people packed the house from the first row to the farthest reach of the balcony. He sidled out from the wings, knees trembling and

Back from his reporting in Hawaii, Mark turned to lecturing to increase his income. He wrote his own advertising copy, enticing people to fill up the hall. This ad ran in a California paper on October 20, 1866.

mouth dry, to be almost knocked down by a roar of applause. Fear melted as he realized these were friends out there, and began to talk to them, handing out information, but taking many funny side paths along the way. Again, as in Nevada, he was a smash hit. He was discovering what he could do best. A friend took over as agent and planned a tour of towns in California and Nevada. Every house was packed; the dollars rolled in.

Back in San Francisco he made a deal to report for the *Alta California* a trip he would take around the world. But first he would go back East by ship. He sailed from San Francisco on the steamer *America*, Captain Ned Wakeman, at noon, December 15, 1866. The first seven letters he sent the *Alta* described the *America*'s adventurous voyage through hurricane seas to a port in Nicaragua. The trip was enlivened by Captain Wakeman's stunning forecastle yarns, told with a defiance of grammar and flights of fancy swearing that filled Mark with admiration. The passengers left the ship and crossed the Isthmus, to catch the steamer *San Francisco* on the Atlantic side. Only a day out at sea, cholera appeared and the passage north became a horror. The sheeted corpses were buried at sea, day after day; when the cholera-stricken ship stopped at Key West, many terrified passengers deserted. Finally, on the morning of January 12, 1867, the *San Francisco* sailed past snow-covered Staten Island, and Mark beheld again vast New York spread out beyond, "encircled with its palisades of masts, and adorned with its hundred steeples."

5

THE INNOCENTS ABROAD

Safe ashore at last, Mark took a room on East Sixteenth Street and began to explore the city he had not seen for thirteen years. He found New York had changed—acres and acres of costly new buildings, a quarter million more souls, another 5,000 men made wealthy while a million were struggling to survive, everything from rent and roast chestnuts to cab rides and champagne much more expensive. But it was still a place where the stranger was lonely.

The city's mood was a wild contrast to sleepy Hannibal:

Every man seems to feel that he has got the duties of two lifetimes to accomplish in one, and so he rushes, rushes, rushes, and never has time to be companionable—never has any time at his disposal to fool away on matters which do not involve dollars and duty and business. . . . There is something about this ceaseless buzz, and hurry, and bustle, that keeps a stranger in a state of unwholesome excitement all the time, and makes him restless and un-easy, and saps from him all capacity to enjoy anything or take a strong interest in any matter whatever—some-

thing which impels him to try to do everything, and yet
permits him to do nothing. . . . This fidgety, feverish
restlessness will drive a man crazy, after a while, or kill
him. I have got to get out of it.

He left New York on a brief visit home to Missouri. Stopping
in St. Louis, he found the women petitioning the legislature for
the right to vote. With thirty-nine lawmakers already won to the
feminist cause, Mark wrote for the *Alta* a piece warning against
female suffrage. He argued that he never wanted to see women—
those "blessed earthly angels"—politicking among "a mob of
shabby scoundrels." It was a widely held view in his time, and
he failed to rise above it. Later he would.

And now, Hannibal. Over five years ago he had left home,
an obscure secretary to his brother Orion, a former printer and
pilot. Now, at thirty-one, he had added miner, reporter, and
lecturer to his professions, and was no longer plain Sam Clemens of Hannibal, but famous Mark Twain—"the Wild Humorist of the Pacific Slope."

Many of his boyhood friends were married. Some had moved
away; others were dead. He gave a lecture to an admiring audience. But he was dismayed by the hard times the town was
suffering. With the decline of steamboating and the end of the
war, the Mississippi Valley was sunk in a depression. Still, he
enjoyed seeing old friends.

Back in New York, he continued his letters to the *Alta*. He
began to like the city again. He knew that if you made your mark
there, you were a made man. So he risked making his platform
debut in New York, at the Cooper Institute. To avoid the ap-
pearance of a flop, his agent papered the great hall with free
tickets. The schoolteachers who grabbed them up roared their
delight at his performance. The papers reviewed his Hawaiian

lecture favorably, so Mark did it in Brooklyn too, and once more in Manhattan.

The big event of these months for Mark was the publication of his first book, *The Celebrated Jumping Frog of Calaveras County and Other Sketches*, at $1.50 a copy. He didn't mind using his *Alta* letters to promote it. He bragged that the cover had "a truly gorgeous gold frog" stamped on it, and that alone was worth the money. He urged all his friends to buy a few copies and place them in Sunday school libraries. While the book made no money, it made friends in high places. The poet and critic James Russell Lowell called it "the finest piece of humorous writing yet produced in America."

While visiting in St. Louis, Mark had seen the announcement of an excursion to the Mediterranean and the Holy Land by the steamship *Quaker City*. The idea for the first transatlantic pleasure cruise from America sprang up in the Reverend Henry Ward Beecher's church. Mark learned that many distinguished people promised to be aboard. His own plan for a trip around the world gave way to this chance to travel in very select company. He got the *Alta* to send him as correspondent. The paper paid the $1,250 passage and promised twenty dollars apiece for his letters. There were a dozen other reporters aboard the side-wheeler when she steamed out of New York on June 8, 1867. A good many of the sixty-seven passengers turned out to be clergy, and most of them considerably older than Mark. This self-chosen elite of the excursion forbade dancing on shipboard because it was sinful. They tried to impose on the cruise a regimen of decorum, dominoes, and devotions. If he had not met more congenial souls, the pleasure cruise might have turned into a funeral excursion without a corpse.

But he did find a batch of carefree younger spirits who helped make the junket both frolic and adventure. What Mark saw and

The miniature portrait of Olivia Langdon which her brother Charlie showed Mark on the Quaker City voyage. "From that day to this," Mark wrote forty years later, "she has never been out of my mind."

did in those five months abroad was transmuted into almost a quarter of a million words. He sent fifty-three letters to the *Alta*, six to the *New York Tribune*, and three to the *New York Herald*. No traveler was ever busier.

The *Quaker City* was a good-size ship for her time, powered by steam and with auxiliary sails. Small as his reputation was, Mark soon became the focus of attention. His humor, his odd manners, and his casual clothing amused the genteel company. Afternoons on deck he read aloud to a little group the letters he was sending to his newspapers. Among the regular listeners entranced by Mark's brilliance was Charles J. Langdon of Elmira, New York, an eighteen-year-old whose wealthy father thought the voyage would be good for his rambunctious son. Charlie and Mark became friends. One September day in the Bay of Smyrna, Charlie invited Mark into his cabin and showed him a miniature portrait of his sister Olivia Langdon. "From that day to this," Mark would write forty years later, "she has never been out of my mind." His long bachelorhood was soon to end.

What Mark meant to do in his letters was to tell the story of the voyage as it happened. His dispatches were an odd mixture—burlesque versions of biblical stories, parodies of the stuffy guidebooks everyone carried abroad, and prose arias about some of the sights, worked up according to a formula. His reports often resorted to comic deflation of such tourist attractions as the Venetian gondola and the Egyptian Sphinx. New in his letters was the emphasis on his own reactions, his own personal experiences. His readers, like his lecture audiences, wanted not so much information about places visited as the pleasure of his company, the public personality Mark Twain.

In mid-November the *Quaker City* was back at its berth in New York. Mark found himself far better known than when he had left. His dispatches from abroad had carried his celebrity to every corner of the country. A day later he was in Washington, working as private secretary to Senator William M. Stewart, an old Nevada acquaintance. This observation post on Washington life was soon wiped out when differences developed with the pompous politician. Nor did Mark's maneuvers produce a hoped-for clerkship for brother Orion. But "hobnobbing with these old Generals and Senators and other humbugs" provided good copy for the newsletters Mark began contributing to the Tribune and Herald in New York and his old papers out West.

What he saw of Washington life etched politics in acid on his mind. "It could probably be shown by facts and figures that there is no distinctly native American criminal class except Congress," he wrote. But he recognized the attraction Washington reporting would have for small out-of-town papers. With another man he formed a syndicate that sent two letters a week to twelve such papers, at a dollar per letter.

The famous writer of the Quaker City letters found every door open to him. A Hartford publisher wrote to inquire if he would like to do a book for them. Mark suggested reworking his Quaker City letters into a travel volume, and asked Rev. Henry Ward Beecher for advice on how to force the best bargain out of the publisher. "I had my mind made up to one thing," he wrote his mother. "I wasn't going to touch a book unless there was money in it, and a good deal of it." He turned down a flat offer of ten thousand dollars cash for the book, with no royalties, and took instead a 5 percent royalty on all copies sold.

But before settling in to work on the book, Mark came up to New York to spend the Christmas holidays with Quaker City friends. Charlie Langdon and his family were in town, too, and Mark was introduced to Olivia, the original of the ivory miniature he had seen in the Bay of Smyrna. "She was slender and beautiful and girlish—and she was both girl and woman," he said. He was thirty-two; she was eleven years younger. On New Year's Day 1868 he dropped in on Olivia Langdon's family at ten in the morning and left the hotel thirteen hours later. On their first date he took Livy and her family to hear Charles Dickens read at Steinway Hall. "Beautiful girl," he wrote his mother and sister. "I am going to spend a few days with the Langdons in Elmira, New York, as soon as I get time."

But covering Capitol Hill, getting started on his book, and lecturing on the West Coast interfered. From now on, lecturing was a solid source of income Mark could always turn to. In a year on the platform (1868–69) he earned over $8,000, a considerable sum then. But, as he wrote to his mother, "I most cordially hate the lecture field. I shudder to think that I may never get out of it." (He never did; he kept on doing it until he died, and not just to make money. He relished himself as a performer. He carefully studied the effects he wanted and learned to produce cataracts of applause just by the way he talked.)

The lecture system started in the early nineteenth century and was in full flower after the Civil War. In the days before radio, films, and television, lecturing was the sole means to bring both information and entertainment to audiences. The skilled lecturer such as Mark Twain was offered as a one-man (or one-woman) show to people eager to see and hear the celebrities of their time. Many eminent Americans made the rounds at an average of about $100 a night for each lecture. The drawing names ranged from the lofty philosopher and poet Ralph Waldo Emerson to the lusty humorist Josh Billings. In between were such notables as the Reverend Henry Ward Beecher, the women's rights advocate Anna Dickinson, editor Horace Greeley, abolitionist Wendell Phillips, and scientist Louis Agassiz. The best agent was ex-newspaperman and abolitionist James Redpath. He took Mark under his wing and earned his 10 percent commission.

To be a lionized lecturer was not all fees and fun. Hotels were often villainously bad—shabby rooms, lumpy beds, dim light, awful food. If Mark stayed in someone's home, he had to submit to an enthusiastic tour of the town in a freezing open buggy, seeing the mayor's home, the public school, the paper mill, the cemetery, the courthouse, and a host of other thrilling wonders—to an obbligato of statistics and dimensions.

What Mark looked like on the platform was captured by a Chicago reporter around this time. Mark was, he wrote, "A thin man of five foot ten [he was actually five foot eight], thirty-five, eyes that penetrate like a new gimlet, nasal prow projecting and pendulous, carrotty, curly hair and mustache, arms that are always in the way, expression dreadfully melancholy. He stares inquisitively here and there, and cranes and cranes his long neck around the house like a bereaved voter who was just coming from the deathbed of his mother-in-law and is looking for a sexton."

It took Mark about six months to prepare the travel book, which he called *The Innocents Abroad*. It came out partly as a journalist's account of what he saw on his travels, partly as autobiography, and partly as fiction, the various kinds of writing shading into one another. A good part of his effort went into composing oratorical flourishes describing historical monuments or celebrated places. Such set pieces were the thing to do. Audiences and critics wanted it, and because they expected it, Mark accommodated them. Such passages were empty flourishes having nothing to do with his firsthand experience. But the book also included his irreverent responses and his comic anecdotes.

Innocents was sold by subscription, a method looked down upon by the literary people of that time. The publisher prepared leaflets, posters, and advertisements touting the coming book as "The Most Unique and Spicy Volume in Existence." A sales force took promotional pieces and sample pages door to door to drum up sales in advance of publication. The book had to be large, lavishly illustrated, and expensively priced. The buyers were primarily small-town and rural readers, far from any bookstore. They would raise a howl if the book delivered didn't give them their money's worth. What they wanted was pleasure, not self-improvement. Mark's way of appealing to them was to move quickly from subject to subject and to shift tone rapidly, because the readers were used to enjoying books only in snatches. The pictures were what they liked to linger over, and in *Innocents* he promised them 234 "beautiful, spirited, and appropriate engravings."

Innocents was published in July, and became a best-seller. (It sold a half-million copies in his lifetime.) The reviewers praised both its eloquence and its humor. What they liked best was Twain's putting himself in the place of the average uncultivated American soaking up Europe and the past. As one paper said, "Twain's book is valuable for pricking many of the bubbles and exploding the humbugs of European travel." William Dean Howells wrote in the *Atlantic Monthly*, "There is an amount of human nature in the book that rarely gets into literature."

It was late August before Mark paid his first visit to the Langdons in Elmira. They lived in a big house built by Livy's father, Jervis Langdon, a wealthy coal dealer. Livy, now twenty-two, had slowly been recovering from a partial paralysis caused by a fall on the ice at sixteen. A genteel young woman, she felt nervous about entertaining an unmarried man, a man ten years her senior, a man known as the Wild Humorist of the Pacific Slope, a man who had written a book. Would he be funny all the time? Would he expect her to be?

The first visit did not turn out to be an ordeal. For two weeks Mark rode, walked, sang, and entertained the Langdons in that lazy drawl that delighted everyone. Before he left he asked the all-important question—and was turned down. Livy would simply be his "sister."

A heavy lecture schedule took Mark away, but letters streamed back and forth and he managed to squeeze in two brief visits. By the end of November, Livy said she was "glad and proud" she loved him. Mark wrote his family that "I love—and *worship*—Olivia L. Langdon of Elmira—& she loves me."

When Jervis Langdon was assured that Mark had a blameless past and could support Livy in the proper style, he gave his consent to the marriage. In February 1869 they became formally engaged, and a year later they were married.

The Langdons were liberals. They had led Elmira abolitionists out of the Presbyterian church in a conflict over slavery and formed a Congregational church. Runaway slaves heading north had found shelter at the Langdons', and men like Garrison, Phillips, and Frederick Douglass were always welcome. Though Livy's background was Victorian, it was hardly orthodox.

Long after, Mark wrote that under Livy's "grave and gentle exterior burned inextinguishable fires of sympathy, energy, devotion, enthusiasm and absolutely limitless affection. She was always frail in body and she lived upon her spirit, whose hopefulness and courage were indestructible."

Although he was a successful lecturer and author of a bestseller, Mark felt that marriage required a more solid financial base. He bought a one-third interest in the *Buffalo Express*, borrowing $12,500 from Jervis Langdon. With Livy he went to Buffalo, expecting to move into a boardinghouse. Instead, his father-in-law surprised him with the grand gift of a completely furnished house on a fashionable street.

For the *Express* Mark wrote editorials, gossip columns, and satires, often spending twelve to fifteen hours at his desk. He took a hand in everything, urging his reporters to "modify the adjectives, curtail their philosophical reflections, and leave out the slang." He toned down the thunder-and-lightning typography and gave the paper a more respectable look.

The son of slaveholders and the ex-Confederate soldier was becoming "de-Southernized." He wrote a powerful editorial against the lynching of blacks, occurring at a rapidly increasing rate in the South. He met Frederick Douglass and supported the black leader's fight against segregation in the schools. He wrote editorials denouncing injustice wherever he found it and never hesitated to name the wrongdoers, no matter how prominent.

Now a great catch in the world of journalism, Mark took up an offer from the *Galaxy* magazine to write a monthly piece on any subject he pleased, for $2,400 a year. His columns blistered many a respectable citizen whose hypocrisy he despised.

That first year in Buffalo began happily. Mark's home life went well. He even accepted—briefly!—such customs as family worship, grace before meals, and Bible readings. Soon, however, it was *his* desires, not Livy's, that ruled the household. He smoked before ladies, lounged about in his slippers, and did and said whatever he pleased. Livy would lecture him on his bad habits; he would confess his sins and go on committing them.

The happy beginning did not last long. Mr. Langdon was stricken with cancer and died in a few months. Then an old school chum of Livy's came to visit, was downed by typhoid fever, and died in their home. These shocks made Livy herself ill, and her first child, Langdon Clemens, was born prematurely.

As the troubles mounted, Mark lost interest in Buffalo and his work on the *Express*. Both he and Livy were ready to move elsewhere. In April 1871 he gave up the *Galaxy* and sold his interest in the *Express*, losing $10,000. It was the end of his career in journalism.

6

AUTHOR! AUTHOR!

In the spring of 1871, Mark, Livy, and the baby moved to Elmira in upstate New York, staying at Quarry Farm, the home of Livy's sister. It was built on a hill, overlooking Elmira and the Chemung River. From now on it would be their favorite summer retreat. He spent the summer completing work on *Roughing It*, the story of his adventures in the West. Elisha Bliss, the Hartford publisher of *Innocents*, had urged Mark to do another travel book. The first one, sold by aggressive house-to-house canvassers, had chalked up huge sales. Both Bliss and Twain thought a new book would surely repeat that success. Mark bragged that he would get 7.5 percent—the biggest royalty ever paid on a subscription book. Perhaps he made so much of the money because he knew most literary men had no use for such books.

Roughing It, too, is narrated by a character called Mark Twain. He carries on the innocent's adventures, but by going backward in time a decade. The story covers the years 1861–66. There is the journey west to Nevada, life in the territory, the San Francisco experience, and the record of the trip to Hawaii.

While the new book did not do as well as *Innocents*, the critics agree it is a better book. Mark's writing was more fluid, more incisive. Amusing as *Innocents* was, it was the product of a journalist hunting for copy. He was not a part of the life he described. In *Roughing It* Mark was working with what he had lived through. As in all his travel books, he padded it (readers wanted big fat books for their money) with some dull stuff and his burlesques. What his audience enjoyed was the contrast drawn between their own workaday reality and the fabulous world of the Western frontier. Mark faced honestly the truth about the violence of the frontier: In Virginia City the first twenty-six graves contained the corpses of murdered men. But he made it palatable to his readers by placing the spotlight not so much on the killers and corpses as on a scared young man's comic reactions to those hard realities.

Mark made his book into more than just another account of Western travel. He showed how the traveler entering this strange region was made into a different person. With the publication of *Roughing It* early in 1872, Mark was at last ready to say his profession was author.

Hartford was to be Mark Twain's first "permanent" home after almost twenty years of wandering. The Connecticut town had won his favor instantly on his first visit, when he came up to settle the contract with Bliss for *Innocents*. He stayed with the Hookers then; Isabella Hooker was Henry Ward Beecher's sister, and she and her husband John were leaders of the town's intellectual life.

Mark thought it the handsomest town he had ever seen— broad, straight streets, simple and shapely homes with landscaped grounds, and thriving businesses in insurance and gun manufacturing. After closing out the house in Buffalo, the Twains moved into the Hooker house in Hartford, renting it until their

*Mark Twain's home was the oddest and most elaborate
in Hartford. Its Gothic turrets, balcony like a pilot house,
porch like a riverboat deck, and lookouts commanding
the best views, were so bizarre they shocked the town.
Today the house is a Mark Twain museum.*

own home was ready in 1874. This was in the Nook Farm literary colony, a hundred-acre tract on the western edge of the city.

The house Mark built was the oddest and most elaborate home in Hartford. It had nineteen large rooms, including a billiard room, a library, and a conservatory, and five baths. He spent $31,000 for the five acres, $70,000 for the house, and $21,000 for furniture. With Gothic turrets, a balcony like a pilothouse, a porch like a riverboat deck, and lookouts commanding the best views, it was a bizarre departure that shocked Hartford for a while. The house was built for comfort and hospitality. Most of Mark's writing was not done there, however, but at Quarry Farm, the summer place in Elmira. The family lived in the house from 1874 to 1891. (Today it is a Mark Twain museum.)

Six months after the move to Hartford, the second child, Susy Clemens, was born. The first child, Langdon, died only ten weeks later, and Susy became the center of attention until another daughter, Clara, was born in 1874, and a third, Jean, in 1880.

Nook Farm was the scene of Mark's happiest and most productive years. The select society kept open house, and conversation about literature and politics flourished. The circle included other writers. Harriet Beecher Stowe, whose *Uncle Tom's Cabin* had made her world famous, lived next door to Mark, and nearby was Charles Dudley Warner, editor of the *Hartford Courant* and of *Harper's*, who wrote travel books, essays, and fiction. Isabella Hooker was an early feminist whose work, said Mark, helped win the only revolution for the emancipation of half a nation that cost no blood. Nearby, too, was the Reverend Joe Twichell, Mark's closest friend for forty years. His congregation of professionals and businessmen Mark called the Church of the Holy Speculators. Mark and Joe debated politics and religion endlessly but affectionately.

The literary lions of Boston and New York found Nook Farm a very congenial stopping place. At large dinners there was "incomparable hilarity," and sometimes the party was up till dawn, enjoying ale, wit, and parlor tricks. Mark liked to dance, sing, and tell stories for the guests.

Whist, skating and sleighing, picnics, long carriage drives, billiards, hikes, bicycling, excursions on the river—these were the recreations of Nook Farm. Servants eased the chores of hospitality, but the continuous social life made creative work difficult. Mark liked to keep three or four books going at the same time, but found he got most of his work done when they were in Elmira for the summer.

As the drain of maintaining a lavish scale of living mounted, Mark confided to a friend that "a life of don't-care-a-damn in a boarding house is what I have asked for in many a secret prayer." But the social round went on; his living expenses for one year soared to $100,000.

Money kept coming in from his books. Still, he needed to go out on the lecture circuit again to pay off his debts. In Boston, at the offices of their agent, James Redpath, Twain met his old friends, the humorists Petroleum V. Nasby and Josh Billings. They all tried out new lectures in the outlying towns before they showed them off at the Boston Music Hall. Here too Mark enjoyed the companionship of William Dean Howells, one of the leading novelists, critics, and editors; the writer-editor Thomas Bailey Aldrich; and James T. Fields, the publisher.

The Boston literary elite failed at first to recognize Mark's quality. He was no traditionalist like them; his new and startling voice was amusing, but they condescended to him as though he were the court jester. Only Howells and a few others recognized a new master early on.

In England Mark's work was completely accepted by the great ones. He decided to make a visit to prepare for another travel

The Twain family on their porch in Hartford

book. He sailed to London alone in the summer of 1872. Another reason for the voyage was to protect his copyright in *Roughing It*. The popular writers of Mark's day suffered from international literary piracy. Theft of a writer's work was common on both sides of the Atlantic. Thieves and bribery were used to snatch proof sheets from the printing houses and binderies of publishers in other countries, for no international copyright law existed then. But British law did grant copyright on a book if it was first published there. So Mark arranged to have *Roughing It* brought out in London before American publication.

At his first luncheon with his British publisher he talked right up to the dinner hour and through it, delighting his hosts. They all went off to the Savage Club afterward, where Mark was warmly welcomed by the explorer Stanley, the actor Henry Irving, and many other notables. They knew an original when they met one.

Mark made many notes about English life while there, but he never wrote the book. Perhaps he liked England too much to be funny about it. Although urged again and again to lecture, he refused. In the fall he began to feel homesick, and wrote Livy that he would go home for now but return with all of them next summer.

Back in Hartford, Mark settled happily into family life. At dinner with the Warners one night, the husbands ridiculed the novels their wives were reading. Challenged to do better, Mark and Warner set to work. Mark had hesitated for some time to try his hand at a novel, although he had in mind a story about James Lampton, his mother's cousin. Perhaps the offer of collaboration was what he needed to push him into his first attempt at a long work of fiction. When Warner approved the idea and agreed to help, Mark wrote the first eleven chapters of the book in a rush. Then Warner did the next twelve. After that they began to rewrite each other's work, until the parts of the novel were fused together. Begun in February, the novel was finished in April. "Warner has worked up the fiction," Mark joked, "and I have hurled in the facts."

The Gilded Age raked to the bone the incredible years following the Civil War, and named the era for posterity. The book is uneven, mixing Warner's sentimental melodrama with Twain's savage satire and burlesque. It was the only contemporary novel to attack the fevered speculation and expose the political muck of that time. The lobbyists, the Wall Street financiers, Washington's political hacks, the boomtowns of the West, the railroad builders, the vulgar new aristocracy of wealth, "the great putty-hearted public" that tolerated the plunder—all fell beneath the axe Mark had been sharpening since that winter of 1867 when he had watched Capitol Hill in action.

Penetrating social satire is half the novel's achievement. The other half is the creation of the immortal visionary Colonel Beriah Sellers, out of cousin James Lampton and Mark's genius. Sellers, the best character in the novel, is a con man brimming over with fantastic schemes to make millions. He is an American type and representative of his period.

Twain and Warner each made $18,000 out of the book. Sold not through the bookstores, but door-to-door like Mark's other books, it rolled through three editions within a month. By the end of 1874, 58,000 copies had been sold. Mark was now a novelist, a creator of characters and an inventor of plots.

It was a good time to return to England, accompanied by his family. On his second visit, he was again entertained royally, and so often that it made Livy ill. They went off to Scotland for a rest and then on to Ireland, finishing with a sightseeing and shopping trip to Paris. This time Mark did lecture in England, giving five successive performances in London and another in Liverpool.

They were home again in October. But within a month Mark was once more in England, briefly this time, to protect his copyright on *The Gilded Age*. In the winter he lectured again for Redpath, and by April he had installed the family at Quarry Farm. There he worked in a separate octagonal study, a small room filled with windows like a pilothouse. In June came the birth of his daughter Clara. Mark took a day off now and then, to play with the children or read with Livy. But most of his time went into making his first solo flight into fiction. *The Adventures of Tom Sawyer*, the book he began, became a children's classic when it appeared two years later. But, as Mark hoped, its appeal has been as great for adults. They enjoy its reminder of what they like to think they were once like themselves.

Tom's beginnings go back to 1870, when Mark explored in diary form the boyhood adventures of a Billy Rogers. Two years later, while in London, he wrote the episode in which Tom tricks his friends into whitewashing the fence. Now, in April 1874 at Quarry Farm, he got the story moving fast. All summer he worked on it, producing fifty pages of manuscript a day, so wrapped up in his dream of boyhood that he was dead to anything else.

When inspiration ran dry, Mark put Tom aside to write a play about Colonel Sellers of *The Gilded Age*, which was produced profitably in New York. With prodigious creative energy he also managed to write his first piece for the *Atlantic Monthly*, edited by his friend Howells. "A True Story" was taken down from Auntie Cord, a black cook at Quarry Farm who had been twice sold as a slave in Virginia. He worked hard to capture her language and personality. (Later, when he wrote *Huckleberry Finn*, he would use something of what she told him.) For it Mark was paid sixty dollars, the highest price the magazine had ever given anyone. He was used to better fees, but he was delighted to find himself in the *Atlantic*.

Urged to contribute again, he told Howells he'd like to do a series "about old Mississippi days of steamboating glory and grandeur as I saw them from the pilot house." The answer was yes, and in a couple of weeks he sent in several chapters.

"Old Times on the Mississippi" appeared in the *Atlantic* from January to July, 1875. The chapters were immediately picked up by newspapers and pirated in book form in Canada. They were a concrete, vivid picture of an apprenticeship to a trade. He had been powerfully moved to write because he would still quit everything else to go piloting—if his wife would only let him. He found the new *Atlantic* audience "the only one I can sit down before in perfect security (for the simple reason that it doesn't require a 'humorist' to paint himself striped and stand on his head every fifteen minutes)." The seven-page articles brought him twenty dollars a page, a rate he deplored. "However," he comforted himself, "the awful respectability of the magazine makes up for it."

In between reliving life on the great river, he skated at Nook Farm with the neighborhood girls, remarking that "there would be a power of fun in skating if you could do it with somebody else's muscles." By January he reported that "the piloting material has been uncovering itself by degrees, until it has exposed such a huge hoard to my view that a whole book will be required to contain it."

But it was years before he took up that unfinished business of the river book. Not until April 1882 did he catch the steamer *Gold Dust* at St. Louis and drift down the Mississippi to New Orleans. There he met his old tutor, Captain Horace Bixby, and made the trip north with him in his new steamboat. At Hannibal, Mark stopped to look around. He spent three happy days there, though he found the town much changed—only the mud was the same. He visited the old places and talked with the gray-

At work in the octagonal study at Quarry Farm, overlooking Elmira, New York. Here in the summertime, Mark found the quiet secluded hours he needed for his best writing.

heads who had been boys and girls with him thirty and forty years before.

Life on the Mississippi appeared in 1883. It was really two books, not one. The *Atlantic* articles are chapters 4 to 20—the marvelous memory of his four prewar years on the river. The last forty chapters are the record of how the river and its towns looked to Mark twenty years later. This part is crammed with statistics, yarns, scenery, essays, an attack on Sir Walter Scott for starting the Civil War, and material lifted hastily from books and newspapers to fill out the book on schedule.

7

TOM
AND
HUCK

With his "inspiration tank," as he called it, filling up again, Mark returned to the story of Tom Sawyer. He worked steadily at it, and in July 1875—about to turn forty—he wrote the final chapter. "It is not a boy's book at all," he wrote Howells. "It will only be read by adults. It is only written for adults." He asked his friend to tell him what he thought of the manuscript, for he would take no other person's judgment, and he was anxious about the first novel he had written alone. Howells sat up all night reading it, and wrote to Mark: "It is altogether the best boy story I ever read. It will be an immense success, but I think you ought to treat it explicitly as a boy's story; grown-ups will enjoy it just as much if you do. . . ."

Mark was delighted. After making some minor changes he had the book published in December 1876. He took the usual precaution of arranging to have it come out first in England. It was now that he began a determined crusade for international copyright law. He appealed to his own country to set a good example to the world by acting justly and refusing to pirate the books of any foreign author. He pointed out publicly how absurdly unjust it was to limit the rights of authors to the literary property they created. If Rockefeller could own his oil wells forever, and a man own his house or his toothbrush forever, why couldn't an author and his heirs own the copyright to his books permanently? He fought hard to get copyright law improved and lived to see some of his goals achieved. Writers owe much to Mark Twain, besides the pleasure and pride they take in his books.

Most of the adventures in *Tom Sawyer* really happened, Mark says in his preface. Some were experiences of his own, others those of his schoolmates. The St. Petersburg of the novel is the Hannibal of his youth. Tom's house was the old Clemens home, and Becky Thatcher's house was a childhood sweetheart's. The school, the church, the cemetery, the island, and the cave can all be traced back to Hannibal. So can the leading characters. Tom himself is made up of Sam Clemens and a couple of his friends, and Huck Finn is drawn from life. What they do and say is harvested from memories recalled long years after. There is no real plot to the book. It is successful Mark Twain looking back fondly on his own boyhood.

The fictional town is made prettier and nicer than the real Hannibal, which was, as Mark once said, "a poor little shabby village." The idyllic setting he provided the story made it "simply a hymn, put into prose to give it a worldly air." Characters he copied from life were modified in the same way. The real people lived on a rough southwestern frontier, and their behavior was shaped by it. In Mark's youth he came close to drowning three times, he saw an abolitionist almost lynched, he witnessed a death by fire, a hanging, an attempted rape, two drownings, and four murders. His memories were softened by time. His book is a nostalgic view of life in a town he idealized. And of course, like many writers, he borrowed ideas from other books and transplanted them into his own. But regardless of where his materials came from, they were transformed by Mark's personality and artistic skill.

Tom Sawyer, too, was sold door-to-door. Its sales started slowly but then topped those of the earlier books, going over two million in Mark's lifetime. Now, long after copyright has ended, it is still his most popular book. It is in print in many editions and languages, and has been seen in several film and television versions.

After Mark finished work on *Tom*, Bret Harte, the Western friend he had first met in San Francisco, proposed that he and Mark should write a play together. Called *Ah Sin*, it was the story of a Chinese laundryman on the Western frontier. It played in Washington and New York in 1877, but made no great stir. Both writers thought of themselves as friendly to the Chinese. Nevertheless, their stereotyped comedy ridiculed the immigrants. The effect was only to strengthen prejudice against the Chinese.

Even while *Ah Sin* was struggling toward disaster, Mark wrote another play about an amateur detective. He dropped it when he realized it was "dreadfully witless and flat." Years later he and Howells had great fun in writing a sequel to the *Sellers* play; it died after a week on the road. He kept trying futilely to dramatize his own novels. Other playwrights were able to adapt his work for commercial success, but his own stagecraft was not equal to the task. He even tried to improve *Hamlet* by adding a burlesque character who strolls through the action making funny comments on it.

In the spring of 1878 the Twain family sailed to Europe for a stay of one or two years. Mark had been investing in some dubious enterprises; none brought any profit. He hoped a new travel book would balance his bank account. In his day Hartford society made the tour of Europe every few years. The fashion piled up household bric-a-brac and swept away provincialism.

The Twains visited Germany, Switzerland, and Italy, and ended with a summer in London, where Mark met the painter

Whistler, the novelist Henry James, and the great Charles Darwin. After seventeen months abroad they returned home in September 1879. Writing A *Tramp Abroad*, the book he patched together from the experiences of this trip, bored him. It is one of his poorer works, though it did bring in useful money.

In Hartford Mark was promptly caught up again in the local life. He expressed his opinions freely. Before the Monday Evening Club he advocated women's suffrage (he had changed his mind), attacked the license of the press, mocked blind loyalty to the Republican Party. For young women of sixteen to twenty, he organized a Saturday Morning Club that met in his home to hear guest speakers. Mark talked to them about temperance, plagiarism, trade unions, and mind reading. In the press he was equally vocal. The *Courant* was always ready to print his views on anything.

He made his mark on the national scene, too, with a speech in Chicago honoring General Grant and a tribute in Boston to Dr. Oliver Wendell Holmes. There were brilliant evenings around his dinner table. Typical of the distinguished guests were his literary friends Howells and Aldrich, the actors Edwin Booth and Sir Henry Irving, and the Civil War heroes Sherman and Sheridan.

There was time to do more than entertain celebrities. A family pleasure was acting in costume the charades Mark invented. He loved to sing the spirituals and jubilee songs he had learned in boyhood, with the children joining in the choruses. And nothing was more fun than reading aloud to the family from the manuscripts he was working on.

For exercise Mark and Joe Twichell took 10-mile walks into the country. Once they started out to walk the 100 miles to Boston but after 28 miles lameness forced them to board a train the rest of the way. He and Twichell bought high-wheelers when the bicycle craze hit and got up at 5 A.M. to take headers on Farmington Avenue.

Baseball was his spectator sport. (Once, when a small boy stole Mark's umbrella from the bleachers, Mark offered a five dollar reward for the umbrella and two hundred dollars for the boy's remains.) Spelling bees exercised his mind at Twichell's church festivals. He spoke against a uniform and arbitrary way of spelling words. "Kow spelled with a large K is just as good as with a small one," he said. "It is better. It gives the imagination a broader field, a wider scope. It suggests to the mind a grand, vague, impressive new kind of a cow."

One of the new books he read aloud from was *The Prince and the Pauper*. When he was thirteen, Mark had found on a Hannibal street a page from a book about Joan of Arc, telling of her prison days. It led him to wide reading in medieval history, and opened the path to novels in the far future. His tank ran dry on *The Prince* too, but after putting it aside for three years he was able to finish it. He got the idea from another children's book about a prince who disguised himself as a blind beggar. He added a beggar disguised as a prince, giving the story a double plot and a new twist. The novel was very different from anything he had done before, a charming romance that pictured old England learning mercy at the hands of two boys, a king and a beggar, twins in spirit.

The book is polite and amiable, not at all in Mark Twain's line, as his Western friends frankly told him. But it pleased Livy, as well as the genteel Hartford circle. They wanted the world to think of him as not just "a humorist joking at everything," but as a sober author making a contribution to American literature. Mark too was pleased with the novel, because he thought it showed he *could* do something dignified and elegant.

It was about this time that Mark began his disastrous involvement with affairs beyond literature. He could always flame with enthusiasm over any gadget that might make a chore easier. The "damned human race" would be saved by the accordion letter file, the fountain pen, or the stylographic pen. In 1871 he won a patent for an invention designed to help a man hold together his shirt, vest, drawers, and pantaloons. Only the model was ever made. Then he patented a scrapbook that did make a bit of money, chiefly because his name was attached to it. His third gimmick was a "memory builder," developed to teach children history dates painlessly. He couldn't sleep as his mind projected the game into a vast scheme that would sweep millions into his pockets. By the time fantasy stopped, the game looked like a cross between an income tax form and a table of logarithms.

He pioneered the use of any tool to ease the author's work. He spent $125 on a primitive typewriter that worked so badly it ruined his morals, he said. Then he bought a better one and mastered it, the first writer to use one professionally. Like Colonel Sellers, he was ready to invest his money in a bewildering variety of other people's inventions—a patent steam generator, a steam pulley, an engraving process, a cash register, a marine telegraph, a mechanical organ, a synthetic food for invalids, a brass-founding process—the list runs to over a hundred.

And, like Colonel Sellers too, he was always falling just short of a smashing success. When young Alexander Graham Bell offered him stock in a new device to carry the human voice on an electric wire, he declined. He couldn't see the telephone as a sound risk. Shortly after he turned down Bell, he put in a telephone wire from his house to the *Courant* office—"the only telephone wire in town," he bragged, "and the first one that was ever used in a private house in the world." It didn't work too well, which multiplied his profanity.

It was in 1881 that he began investing in a new typesetting machine being developed in Hartford. As an old printer, he could see the value of the invention. He put $5,000 into the Paige typesetter and forgot about it. But not for long. Year after year he poured more money into refinements on a machine that had 18,000 separate parts. Long years later the tinkering was still going on, the money still pouring out. Mark ignored reports of other inventors busy on the same type of machine. By 1890 the Paige was swallowing $4,000 a month, and wiping out Livy's inheritance, too. Mark tried to induce millionaire friends to share the investment, but none would. By 1891 nearly $200,000 had gone down the drain, and Mark was almost frantic at the threat of financial disaster.

Of course family and life went on all through this trouble. Early in the 1880s Mark met and liked at once George Washington Cable, like himself a Southern writer and a marvelous talker. Cable had just come out of obscurity with two books about Louisiana life that portrayed blacks sympathetically. He stayed with the Twains while lecturing in Hartford. In 1884 the two men went out on the road for four months, billed as "Twins of Genius." Each gave readings from his own work. The tour excited great public interest, netting Mark $15,000. But tension grew, for Cable was too penny-pinching and pious for Mark. But Mark helped loosen up Cable, who soon was able to enjoy the theater, tolerate cardplaying, drink Scotch, and travel on Sundays.

Like Mark, Cable never gave up his hatred of social injustice. He was forced to move from the South because of his subversive defense of the black people's civil rights. With Twain he shared the distinction of pioneering in the literature of Southern realism. Perhaps the brilliant mind that produced the dramatic

1 page book – program.

Sellers, materializer

"   Swearing – pho.

This a gov'ment,

Jumping Frog,

Gov. Gardner.

Tom Story just as I heard it.

Blue – jays –   Fanshaw

Boy-fight.

Raft fight.

Gadsby's Hotel

DE – parted

Cable ——— 15 minutes

Sollerman —

Huns Boote   } 10 m
Huns Braine } 4 "

Cable —— Songs ——— 20
(or songs)

Tragic Tale ——— 10
Situation ——— 15
Night ride ——— 13
Jumping Frog ——— 20
                   10

Hang it, Huck, ef I could
cleck de intrust I would
let de principal go."

1 hour for myself, 10 m
for preliminary delay; 40
m for Cable. ——— 1.50.

Facing page: *Mark Twain of Missouri and
George Washington Cable of Louisiana, billed
as the "Twins of Genius" during their 1884–85 tour*
Above: *pages from Mark's notebook during the tour.
Twain blocked out his own material (on the left)
and the program's timing (on the right).*

novels and fearless essays (*The Silent South* and "The Negro Question"), exposing the social and moral problems of his region, helped shape Mark's thinking in that brief but intense association. *Huck Finn* may owe something to Cable.

That novel, *The Adventures of Huckleberry Finn*, appeared in 1885, the year Mark turned fifty. Mark's greatest, it had been born in 1876, as "another boy's book," to follow *Tom Sawyer.* Mark wrote 400 pages, maybe a third of the novel, then dropped it. *Huck* stirred briefly to life in 1880, then subsided. The trip on the Mississippi in 1882 freshened Mark's interest in the little river rat's adventures. And in August 1883 he told Howells he had written nearly 900 pages in a very brief period, working all day long six days a week. By the spring of 1884 proofs were coming from the printer. In December and January the *Century* magazine printed chapters from the book. In February the canvassers were able to rush 40,000 copies of *Huck* to customers who had ordered in advance.

"You don't know about me without you have read a book by the name of *The Adventures of Tom Sawyer*, but that ain't no matter." With these first words from Huckleberry Finn, the reader enters a stream of delightful language that floats him through a score of picaresque adventures shared by the boy and the runaway slave Jim. Twain's radical use of the common speech and his fresh vision of landscape are caught in Huck's report of life on a river raft:

Two or three days and nights went by; I reckon I might say they swum by, they slid along so quiet and smooth and lovely. Here is the way we put in the time. It was a monstrous big river down there—sometimes a mile and a half wide; we run nights, and laid up and hid daytimes; soon as night was most gone we stopped navigating and tied up—nearly always in the dead water under a towhead; and then cut young cottonwoods and willows, and

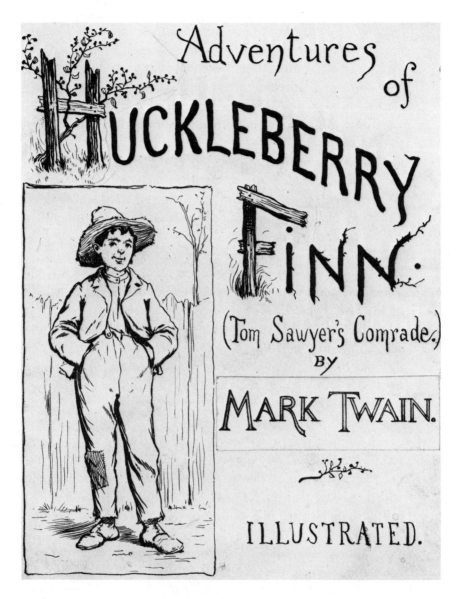

*The original design
for the book's cover*

*hid the raft with them. Then we set out the lines. Next we slid
into the river and had a swim, so as to freshen up and cool off;
then we set down on the sandy bottom where the water was about
knee-deep, and watched the daylight come. Not a sound anywheres—perfectly still—just like the whole world was asleep, only
sometimes the bullfrogs a-cluttering, maybe. The first thing to
see, looking away over the water, was a kind of dull line—that
was the woods on t'other side; you couldn't make nothing else
out; then a pale place in the sky; then more paleness spreading
around; then the river softened up away off, and warn't black
any more, but gray; you could see little dark spots drifting along
ever so far away—trading-scows, and such things; and long black
streaks—rafts; sometimes you could hear a sweep screaking; or
jumbled-up voices, it was so still, and sounds come so far; and
by and by you could see a streak on the water which you know
by the look of the streak that there's a snag there in a swift cur-
rent which breaks on it and makes that streak look that way; and
you see the mist curl up off of the water, and the east reddens
up, and the river, and you make out a log cabin in the edge of
the woods, away on the bank on t'other side of the river, being a
wood-yard, likely, and piled by them cheats so you can throw a
dog through it anywheres; then the nice breeze springs up, and
comes fanning you from over there, so cool and fresh and sweet
to smell on account of the woods and the flowers; but sometimes
not that way, because they've left dead fish laying around, gars
and such, and they do get pretty rank; and next you've got the
full day, and everything smiling in the sun, and the songbirds
just going it!*

*A little smoke couldn't be noticed now, so we would take some
fish off of the lines and cook up a hot breakfast. And afterwards
we would watch the lonesomeness of the river, and kind of lazy
along, and by and by lazy off to sleep. Wake up by and by, and
look to see what done it, and maybe see a steamboat coughing*

along up-stream, so far off towards the other side you couldn't tell nothing about her only whether she was a stern-wheel or side-wheel; then for about an hour there wouldn't be nothing to hear nor nothing to see—just solid lonesomeness. . . .

Sometimes we'd have that whole river all to ourselves for the longest time. Yonder was the banks and the islands, across the water; and maybe a spark—which was a candle in a cabin window; and sometimes on the water you could see a spark or two— on a raft or a scow, you know; and maybe you could hear a fiddle or a song coming over from one of them crafts. It's lovely to live on a raft. We have the sky up there, all speckled with stars, and we used to lay on our backs and look up at them, and discuss about whether they was made or only just happened. Jim he allowed they was made, but I allowed they happened; I judged it would have took too long to make so many. Jim said the moon could 'a' laid them; well, that looked kind of reasonable, so I didn't say nothing against it, because I've seen a frog lay most as many, so of course it could be done. We used to watch the stars that fell, too, and see them streak down. Jim allowed they'd got spoiled and was hove out of the nest.

Huckleberry Finn got the greatest advance publicity of any book by Mark up to that time. And much of it was due to his own efforts. An old hand at journalism, he knew how powerful a mechanism the press was in shaping public opinion. Long before the public relations trade was founded, Mark "worked the newspapers" (his own phrase) to call attention to his books and lectures and to influence the treatment they got. He quickly learned how important it is to get publicity for a book the moment it is published.

As the best salesman of his own books, he promoted *Huck Finn* by reading from it while on tour with Cable. When the Concord Library in Massachusetts banned the book, calling it "the veriest trash . . . rough, coarse, and inelegant," the press took sides in a censorship fight. That put *Huck* on the front pages. "A rattling tiptop puff" from Concord's "moral icebergs," Mark commented. "They have expelled Huck from their library as 'trash suitable only for the slums.' That will sell 25,000 copies for us sure."

The book was off to a great sale. But the critics were indifferent or cold. The *Century* was the only magazine to review it. None of the country's major newspapers did. Some of them editorialized that Mark's day as a writer was done. The book was too vulgar for the critics of that genteel age. (The book did not surpass *Tom Sawyer* in sales, but is gaining on it year by year.) Today *Huck* is considered Twain's masterpiece, and one of the world's great novels. But a hundred years ago both critics and most general readers did not realize that a masterpiece had been created. Neither did Mark himself.

What is it that makes *Huck* unique? The novel is the story of Huck Finn, the thirteen-year-old son of the town drunkard of St. Petersburg, Missouri. Neglected, abused, and half-starved, he decides to run away. He wants to escape his father's beatings and the attempts by some good women to "sivilize" him. On an island in the Mississippi he meets the runaway slave, Jim. They join up to float "free and easy" on a raft for hundreds of miles down the river. Huck and Jim have a series of adventures with many people and in many towns along the way. They are fugitives from the law and live by their wits. In the end—but read it yourself, if you haven't already.

There were lots of adventure stories before *Huck*, but Mark's was different. Why? Because he had the inspired idea of letting Huck tell his own story in his own style. It is the living Huck— with his special experience and way of life, his own unschooled view of the world—who speaks to the reader in his own voice. The river and the life along its shores are seen and felt by Huck in his own unselfconscious way, with his fresh eye for concrete facts and details. It is the sound of his voice the reader hears. He gives us the imperfect world as he finds it.

Huck's language was never before used in a long work of fiction. It is Huck's point of view that Mark Twain keeps to throughout the story. It took great daring and enormous skill for Mark to establish so convincing an illusion. His use of the common speech as the medium to tell the story was new and revolutionary in technique. By doing this, Mark took himself off-stage and made his story entirely dramatic. Everything he wanted to say he said within the limits of a voice and vocabulary not his own.

Huckleberry Finn speaks out against stupid conformity and for the freedom and independence of the individual. Huck helps Jim to escape from slavery, and in a famous scene Huck's spontaneous self is placed in opposition to his acquired conscience, to the prejudices and values of the society he was raised in. When his true self triumphs over his false conscience the emotional climax of the book is reached.

But that *Huck* is not a perfect novel, few would deny. In the last long section of the book Huck accepts Tom Sawyer's leadership and Jim becomes degraded. Mark Twain seems to have lost track of what he was doing and burlesques his own plot. In Tom Sawyer's silly scheming "Jim is reduced to the status of a 'darkey' in a minstrel show," as the critic Henry Nash Smith put it. The reader feels badly sold out. The book is a strong voice against racism, but at the same time some passages mirror the values of the racist society Mark was raised in. Mark could praise the stereotypes of blackface minstrelsy while opposing the inhumane treatment of black Americans. In Huck's controversial use of the term "nigger," the novel—and other writing by Twain—shows that like Huck, Mark was trapped in the bigotry of his day and could not always rise above it.

Yet often he did. In the same year that *Huck* was published, Twain arranged to pay the expenses of one of the first black students at Yale Law School. In his letter to the dean, which recently came to light, Mark said: "I do not believe I would very cheerfully help a white student who would ask a benevolence of a stranger, but I do not feel so about the other color. We have ground the manhood out of them, & the shame is ours, not theirs, & we should pay for it."

Commenting on the letter, Professor Sterling Stuckey, who is black and teaches Twain in his course on the arts and history at Northwestern University, said: "It's a clear condemnation of the larger society for what it had done and was in the process of doing to black people. It couldn't be a clearer, more categorical indictment of racism in American life, and I'm not at all surprised to find that it came from Twain."

The law student Mark helped, Warner T. McGuinn, was financed by Twain until he graduated in 1887. He became a lawyer in Baltimore, where he was elected twice to the City Council, and successfully challenged a city ordinance that mandated segregated housing. Twain continued to support a number of other promising black students at various colleges.

Huck had a powerful literary effect upon writers of the twentieth century. Ernest Hemingway's tribute is familiar: "All modern American literature comes from one book by Mark Twain called *Huckleberry Finn*." William Faulkner said that Mark Twain was the father of Sherwood Anderson, who in turn was "the father of my generation of writers and the tradition of American writers which our successors will carry on." And the poet T. S. Eliot wrote that Twain was one of those rare writers who "discovered a new way of writing, valid not only for themselves but for others."

8

A CONNECTICUT YANKEE

Mark turned fifty the year *Huck* was published. Back then, when the human life span was much shorter, fifty was a ripe old age, a time to enjoy so successful a career. But for the great humorist life was turning out to be anything but unadulterated fun. "I have a badgered, harassed feeling a good part of my time," he wrote to his mother. "It comes mainly from business responsibilities and annoyances." Huge sums were sucked into schemes that would never pay off. And more went into supporting an ever-more-lavish scale of living.

Spending more and more, he needed to earn more and more. From writing books he took to publishing books, his own and others. His publisher Bliss had died in 1880, and Mark had taken to financing his own books under J. R. Osgood's imprint. By 1884 he had his own publishing house, Charles L. Webster and Company, named for the nephew who managed it. *Huck Finn* was the new firm's first subscription book, and a grand success.

The next book made publishing history. It was the *Memoirs* of Ulysses S. Grant, long a friend of Mark's. To meet large debts after he left the presidency, Grant began to write his Civil War recollections. Mark offered to publish them and Grant finished them in his last days, dying of cancer. Within a year Grant's widow received royalties totaling $350,000, the largest sum ever paid an author up to that time.

Although Grant's administration had been tainted by the greed and corruption satirized in *The Gilded Age*, Mark did not turn his back on a friend. He himself fell prey to the dream of easy money. But with the same gusto he gave to his get-rich-quick schemes, he heaved bricks at the Vanderbilts and Rockefellers. He liked success and delighted in the comforts wealth provided. Yet he could not stand the worship of money, nor the sacrifice of human values to the getting of it.

Although he was a clown and satirist all along, there was rage beneath the laughter. In the 1870s and 1880s his hatred of injustice found even fuller voice. When Jay Gould, the notorious financial manipulator, ruined thousands by his swindles, and died leaving $72 million, Mark wrote this acid comment:

> *Jay Gould was the mightiest disaster which has ever befallen this country. The people had* desired *money before his day but he taught them to fall down and worship it. They had respected men of means before his day, but along with this respect was joined the respect due to the character and industry which accumulated it. But Jay Gould taught the entire nation to make a god of the money and the man, no matter how the money might have been acquired.*

Presidential elections brought Mark into political campaigning. He judged candidates not on their party but on their stand on issues. To be loyal to country or party is well, he said, "but as certainly a man's first duty is to his own conscience and honor— the party or the country come second to these, and never first. . . . It is not parties that make or save countries or that build them to greatness—it is clean men, clean ordinary citizens, rank and file, the masses."

He couldn't tolerate either the hypocrisy that claimed poverty was a blessing in disguise or the slander that poverty was the fault of the poor. In his years on the Mississippi, he had supported the river pilots who organized a union and won higher pay. When the Knights of Labor rose to strength in the 1880s, a move to outlaw the industrial union as a subversive organization swung into action. Mark publicly defended unions, saying they were here to stay. The unionized workman is doing "the most righteous work that was ever given into the hand of man to do; and he will do it," Mark said.

As he was declaring himself, Mark was working on a new novel that reflected his concern for social justice. The story of *A Connecticut Yankee in King Arthur's Court* was meant to contrast the daily life of King Arthur's day with the life of Mark's time. Issued in 1889, it was his first book in five years, and badly needed by his publishing business. At its heart was a plea for human rights over property rights, for social progress over selfish interests. Many readers slid right past the theme because they were laughing at Mark's broad burlesque of kings and aristocrats. The delightful fantasy used a time warp to sweep a Yankee mechanic back into the days of chivalry. When Howells read it he said, "It's a mighty great book and it makes my heart burn with wrath. It seems that God didn't forget to put a soul in you. He shuts most literary men off with a brain, merely."

Yankee was much more widely reviewed than *Huck*. Some critics praised "the great American humorist" for treating the themes of human equality, unjust laws, the power of the rich, and the abuse of the poor. Others attacked him for being preachy and ignorant. The novel sold slowly at first but over the years won great popularity.

After *Yankee* came out, rheumatism lodged in Mark's arm,

making it difficult to write. He tried dictating into a phonograph until the pain subsided. When both his mother and Livy's died in 1890, and his daughter Jean fell ill, he was so depressed that he wrote a friend, "Merry Christmas to you, and I wish to God I could have one myself before I die." He thought perhaps the European baths would ease his rheumatism. (Livy too suffered from it, and was also bothered by heart trouble.) In June 1891 the family sailed for Europe, leaving the Hartford home never to live in it again. They planned a long stay abroad, hoping to find better health and lower living costs.

For nine years the Twains made their home abroad. They moved restlessly through France, Germany, Italy, Switzerland, Austria, England, and Sweden. For the first few years, Mark ferried back and forth across the Atlantic to see if the Paige type-setter would miraculously rescue his sinking publishing business. The long economic depression that began in 1893 was the final disaster. Now nothing but his pen and his voice—no small assets—would support his family.

In their European rovings Mark's popularity, as always, attracted brilliant and amusing company. His widely translated books were read everywhere. The royal courts, the embassies, the universities, the press sought him out in every city. When the German emperor invited him to dinner, Mark's daughter Jean said, "Papa, the way things are going, pretty soon there won't be anybody for you to get acquainted with but God."

Once, traveling down the Rhone in a flat-bottomed boat, without Livy along, he viewed "the vast and idiotic" ruins of castles built long ago on the high hills by princes and Crusaders. The moldy walls and broken towers made him think of how "the Romans displaced the Gauls, the Visigoths displaced the Romans, the Saracens displaced the Visigoths, the Christians displaced the Saracens, and it was these pious animals," he wrote Livy, "who built these strange lairs and cut each other's throats in the name and for the glory of God, and robbed and burned and slew in peace and war; and the pauper and the slave built churches, and the credit of it went to the Bishop who racked the money out of them. These are pathetic shores, and they make one despise the human race."

Both abroad and on his occasional trips home, hardly a day passed without a reporter seeking his opinions. On the street, in a train or on a ship, at work or on holiday, it made no difference. He always had to have his wit and wisdom on tap for a thirsty public. He gave hundreds and hundreds of interviews but was hardly ever satisfied with the results. The reader, he felt, rarely knew "where I was in earnest and where I was joking, or whether I was joking altogether or in earnest altogether." Naked talk in print simply didn't convey his manner or tone.

With all that attention focused on him, he stayed natural. He enjoyed the universal applause without pretending to be humble.

The year 1894 ended with both Mark's publishing house and the Paige machine dead and buried. He lost $60,000 in his Webster Company, and Livy $65,000. The company owed ninety-five creditors about $1,000 apiece. The Panic of 1893 cut off Livy's income from her inheritance. And Mark's royalties almost vanished. To celebrate their silver wedding anniversary, Mark could give Livy only a five-franc piece. He pushed on with his new book, *Joan of Arc*, and finished it in Paris.

Their debts sickened both Mark and Livy. They were determined to pay back every cent. How? Mark decided on a lecture tour around the world, with a book to come out of it as an extra dividend.

In May 1895 the family went back to Quarry Farm to rest and prepare for the tour. He hated to make the worldwide journey alone. Livy and Clara decided to go with him. Susy and Jean would stay with their aunt in Elmira. In July their train

A *sketch from* Puck *shows Twain
on the lecture platform.*

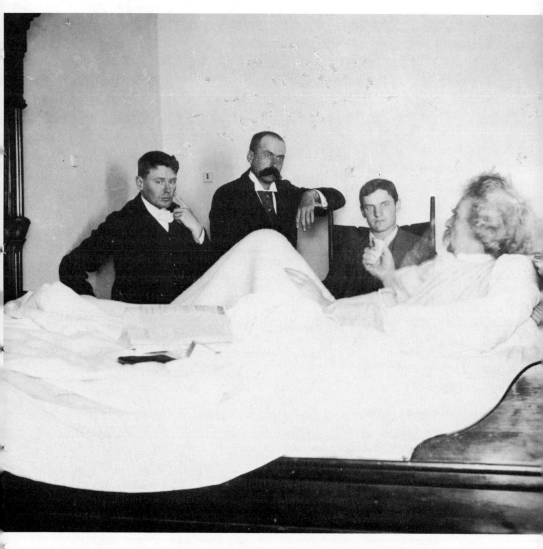

*During his worldwide lecture tour of 1895, Mark gives
a leisurely interview to reporters in Vancouver, Canada.*

headed west, leaving Susy alone on the station platform, waving good-bye.

Before leaving, Mark had placed his affairs in the hands of Henry H. Rogers, a multimillionaire friend who was a chief executive of Standard Oil. Rogers was known in the 1890s as the handsomest and most ruthless pirate who ever flew a flag in Wall Street. He had long admired Mark's work, and he loved the man. Responding to the appeal for help, he dragged Mark out of his troubles without injuring his pride. He negotiated settlements with Mark's creditors and arranged for *Harper's* to take over all Mark's copyrights and become his exclusive publisher, assuring him of an annual income of $25,000. The fees from the lecture tour were sent home to Rogers regularly and used to repay the creditors. By the end of 1898, adding book earnings to the pot, the creditors had all been paid 100 cents on the dollar.

The grand tour began with a lecture in Cleveland and ended with one in Capetown, South Africa. Mark "lectured and robbed and raided" for thirteen months, as he put it. It was hard work, especially with Mark crippled by carbuncles. In one thirty-eight-day stretch, he gave twenty-four lectures in twenty-two cities. For readings he relied mainly on *Roughing It* and *Innocents Abroad*, sometimes throwing in *Tom* and *Huck*. Everywhere—Australia, New Zealand, Ceylon, India, South Africa—houses were packed and records broken. He was a kind of traveling exhibit for American culture. At Johannesburg for eight nights running, crowds jammed the hall, overran the stage, and fought to get through the closed doors. But expenses were too high to make the trip a great financial success.

From South Africa they sailed for England. It was August 1896. Three days out a cablegram told Mark that his daughter Susy had died at home. Only twenty-four, she had been seized with meningitis, a brain infection. She was his favorite, the child most like himself. "It is a mystery of our nature," he wrote, "that a man, all unprepared, can receive a thunder-stroke like that and live."

Susy's death brought the deep pessimism of his nature to the surface. His bitterness appeared more openly. That winter in London he turned to work to escape his sorrow and repay what debts still remained. But he did his work "without purpose and without ambition," he told Howells, "only for the love of it."

9

THE LAST YEARS

Months after Susy's death, Mark settled down to finish his last travel book, *Following the Equator*. It dealt with his trip around the world. He was indifferent to everything but work. It puzzled him that in his bleakness he could still write comedy and find pleasure in doing it. He saw only a few close friends while he kept grinding away at the book—the longest he had yet written. He finished it in the spring of 1897. When it appeared in the fall it did well, enabling him to pay off his final debts.

His financial disaster was behind him now, but he seemed not to have learned anything from it. Soon he was dickering with an Austrian inventor for the American rights to a wonderful carpet-pattern machine that he was sure would bring in millions. Luckily, his financial advisor Rogers squelched the grand scheme. He invested Mark's earnings more wisely in stocks that assured a comfortable income.

The tide of Mark's fortunes began to turn. He felt peace of mind once again. Livy's gloom lifted for the first time since Susy's death, and Mark no longer had nightmares about leaving his family poor. Now, he said, he could spend six cents for his cigars, not four-and-a-half! The Twains went back to living in elaborate suites in deluxe hotels.

In the fall of 1900 the family returned to America. They had been abroad for almost ten years; Mark came home to a hero's welcome. They rented a furnished house at 14 West Tenth Street in New York. Big-city life was essential to Mark now; he could no longer live in Hartford. Besides, it held too many memories of happiness forever gone. His new home was immediately the most popular place in town. Guests dropped in at all hours, and the phone rang day and night.

Honors came fast. Oxford University in England and Yale gave him doctoral degrees. Awarded another at the University of Missouri, he said, "If I am not called at least 'Doc' from now on, there will be a decided coolness." He took this occasion to stop off at Hannibal, visiting his old home and posing for photographs standing at the front door, while the townsfolk admired their native son. Dozens of people told the reporters they were the originals of Tom and Huck and Becky. When he took the pulpit in a crowded church, the sudden rush of feeling made him stand silent for a long moment until he could speak without his voice breaking.

To be lionized was a pleasure for a time, but it wore him down. He spoke at so many luncheons and dinners that he had no time left to write. Everyone begged him to comment on everything. His daughter Clara said it puzzled her how her father "could manage to have an opinion on every incident, accident, invention, or disease in the world." The man once taken lightly as a clown was now being taken seriously as a sage. His innumerable photographs crowded the pages of the press, making the man in the white suit with the thick shock of white hair an instantly recognized figure wherever he went. His was the legendary American pattern of the rise from rags to riches. He be-

Twain at his favorite diversion

came a celebrity whose drawling opinions and peculiar mannerisms made great copy. "I doubt if there is another man on earth whose name is more familiar," said the writer and editor Thomas Bailey Aldrich. A modern student of his public image said that Twain became "the most photographed subject or object since the invention of the camera."

While he enjoyed his celebrity, Mark knew how misleading and fragile public opinion could be. It is not "the Voice of God," he reminded himself. Yet he risked his fame by putting it to work for humane causes. In these years he became the even-more-outspoken critic of "the usual depravities and baseness and hypocrisies and cruelties that make up civilization." He despised imperialism's adventures wherever they occurred. In the far corners of the world, he had himself seen what the expansionist powers were doing to the weaker countries of Africa, to the Filipinos, to the Chinese. Journeying across South Africa in 1896 Mark had sided with the Africans against the English and the Boers, and three years later had stood by the Boers in their resistance to British invasion. When the war with Spain began in 1898, Mark had at first supported what he thought was an effort to free Cuba. But early in 1900, with the United States now fighting in the Philippines, he came to feel, as he told the *New York Herald*, that "we do not intend to free but to subjugate the people. We have gone there to conquer, not to redeem. It should, it seems to me, be our pleasure and duty to make those people free and let them deal with their own domestic questions in their own way. And so I am an anti-imperialist. I am opposed to having the eagle put its talon on any other land."

In the case of the Boxer Rebellion, Mark said, "My sympathies are with the Chinese. They have been villainously dealt with by the sceptered thieves of Europe, and I hope they will drive all the foreigners out and keep them out for good. We have no more business in China than in any other country that is not ours."

He joined the Anti-Imperialist League, which his friend Howells had helped to form. In 1901, at the risk of losing some book sales, he published an article called "To the Person Sitting in Darkness." It was an attack upon the imperialists of all nations that brought him both furious condemnation and high praise.

His friend Rev. Joe Twichell had urged him to be silent, but Mark angrily replied: "I can't understand it! You are a public guide and teacher, Joe, and are under a heavy responsibility to men, young and old; if you teach your people—as you teach me—to hide their opinions when they believe their flag is being abused and dishonored, lest the utterance do them and a publisher damage, how do you answer for it to your conscience?"

To the bill of particulars he drew up against the great powers for the way they exercised their "unwilling" missions in South Africa, China, and the Philippines, Mark now added the crime of King Leopold's rule in the Congo. The Belgian monarch had taken control of the lives of twenty million Africans. Investigators revealed that he had dispossessed the people and built a huge fortune upon their forced labor.

Out of the protests of explorers and missionaries came a Congo Reform Association that asked Mark to lend his voice to the cause of the Congo people. He wrote "King Leopold's Soliloquy," an article no American magazine would print. It reached the public as a pamphlet, with atrocity photographs issued by the Congo reform groups in America and England. Americans with investments in the Congo tried to suppress distribution of the pamphlet and editorial comment on it. But Mark's voice rang out, and counted in the worldwide clamor that in 1908 helped bring Leopold's atrocities in the Congo to an end. He was like

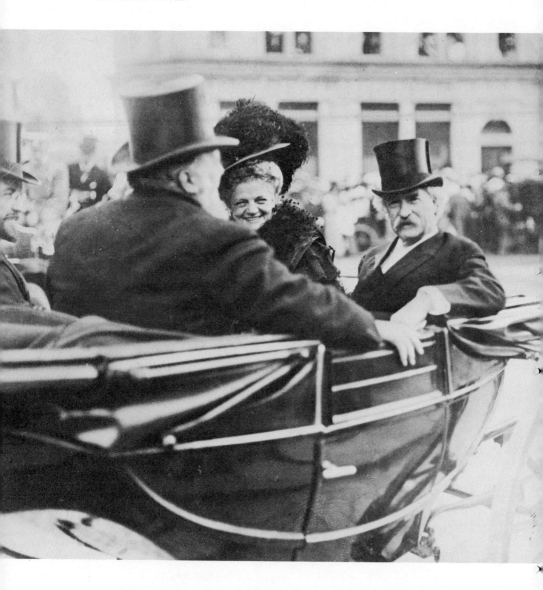

Treated like the king of New York in his last years,
Mark was photographed everywhere and all the time.
Here he rides down Fifth Avenue with friends.

a second Tom Paine, someone said, "vigilant for liberty everywhere."

Leaving Tenth Street, the family settled at Riverdale on the Hudson, close by the city. Mark joined an independent citizens' group to campaign for the defeat of Tammany Hall in the New York elections. A stinging speech he gave reached hundreds of thousands of voters in pamphlet form and contributed to the victory of the reform ticket. One day he marched in a suffragist parade on Fifth Avenue, glad to link himself to women's struggle for the vote.

For recreation Mark took sailing expeditions on Henry Rogers's yacht to Nova Scotia or the West Indies. Summering in Maine in 1902, Livy became seriously ill with both asthma and an organic heart condition. She collapsed and could not be taken back to Riverdale until October. In the fall she was so sick that the doctors would not let Mark see her except for a few minutes a day. In December Jean developed pneumonia and came close to dying. They spent the summer at Quarry Farm, and when the doctors suggested that a milder climate might help Livy, they took a villa in Italy in the hills above Florence. That winter Livy seemed to improve a bit, but as spring began Mark could tell she had given up. On the evening of June 5, 1904, sitting upright in bed, with an oxygen tube in her mouth, she died.

At his age Mark came to expect the death of family or friends almost daily. Besides Livy, he lost his sister Pamela and Molly Clemens, his brother's widow, in 1904 (Orion had died in 1897). Livy's death deeply shocked Mark's daughters. Jean had her first epileptic seizure within a year and would never be well again. (She died five years later.) Clara had a nervous breakdown. After Livy's burial in Elmira, Mark moved to 21 Fifth Avenue, at the corner of Ninth Street. He resumed work on portions of the autobiography he had begun long ago in the 1870s. The *North American Review* liked the chapters he showed them, and paid handsomely to publish them. With the money he bought 248 acres near Redding, Connecticut, and had Howells's architect son John build him an Italianate villa. Clara named it Stormfield.

The autobiography, which he dictated mornings to a secretary, was done piecemeal, in random form. He talked about whatever interested him that day, and carried it wherever his mood turned him. A kind of free association of ideas shaped it. In the afternoons he would go over the typescript and polish it, but without losing the casual quality that made for good talk. For the next two-and-a-half years he kept at it, living in a "creative ecstasy of talking, talking, talking," as his biographer Justin Kaplan wrote. "Throughout the biography is the talk, the like of which, Howells said, we shall never know again—and we never have. As a record of magnificent talk, magical, hilarious, savage, and tender, the autobiography is a major work, Mark Twain's last, a sprawling and shapeless masterpiece whose unity is the accent and rhythm and attack of his voice."

The dictation went on until 1908, when Mark moved into his new home at Redding. Now, he said, he had entered "upon a holiday whose other end is in the cemetery." At Stormfield he played billiards and hearts hour after hour, took walks, or rode about the countryside in the old carriage Jervis Langdon had given him as a wedding present. He gave one more performance as a benefit for the free library he donated to the town.

Mornings he stayed in bed, writing letters or essays. His daughter Jean came to live with him and worked as his secretary. In October 1909 Clara and the pianist Ossip Gabrilowitsch were married at Stormfield. Two days before Christmas, Jean died; she had an epileptic seizure in her bath and drowned. Mark set down his account of what she had meant to him; then said, "I shall never write any more."

Four months later, on April 21, 1910, he died.

CHRONOLOGY

1867–69	Reporting and lecturing.
1869	*The Innocents Abroad* published.
1870	Married Olivia Langdon, February 2; edited *Buffalo Express*.
1871	Moved to Hartford; lecture tours.
1872	*Roughing It*; lecture tour in England.
1873	*The Gilded Age*; lectures in England.
1876	*The Adventures of Tom Sawyer*.
1878–79	Long stay in Europe.
1880	*A Tramp Abroad*.
1882	*The Prince and the Pauper*.
1883	*Life on the Mississippi*.
1884–85	Platform readings with George W. Cable; established publishing house, Charles L. Webster & Co.
1885	*Adventures of Huckleberry Finn*.
1888	Honorary M.A. degree conferred by Yale.
1889	*A Connecticut Yankee in King Arthur's Court*.
1891–95	Lived in Europe.
1894	Paige typesetter declared a failure; Webster Co. in bankruptcy.
1894	*Pudd'nhead Wilson*.
1896	Daughter Susy died, August 18.
1897–1900	Lived in Vienna and London.
1897	*Following the Equator*.
1900	*The Man That Corrupted Hadleyburg and Other Stories*.
1901	Litt.D. conferred by Yale.
1902	LL.D. conferred by University of Missouri.
1903	Took family to Italy for wife's health.
1904	Olivia Clemens died in Italy, June 5.
1907	Litt.D. conferred by Oxford.
1908	Moved to Stormfield, near Redding, Connecticut.

1909   Daughter Jean Clemens died, December 23.
1910   Mark Twain died at Stormfield, April 21; buried
            at Elmira, New York.

BIBLIOGRAPHY

Mark Twain's popularity with the reading public is constant. Every generation of new readers enjoys his writing. A list of his books now in print can be checked in any school or public library. Much of his work is in the public domain, and new editions in paperback of the most widely read books—*Tom Sawyer, Huckleberry Finn, Life on the Mississippi, The Prince and the Pauper*—can be found in almost any bookstore.

Probably more research has been published on Twain than on any other American writer, which is why I have not attempted to select a short list. (See Thomas A. Tenney's *Mark Twain: A Reference Guide*, G. K. Hall, 1977, which records and annotates everything important up to then.) Instead, I indicate some kinds of writing about the man and his work you might want to look into.

Readers who desire autobiographical material can go to the *Autobiography* itself, of course (not to be trusted for facts), and to collections of Twain's letters addressed to various people, his speeches, notebooks, and journals. There are scores of books about his life. They range from the massive pioneer work in three volumes, Albert Bigelow Paine's *Mark Twain: A Biography* (Harper, 1912), to Justin Kaplan's *Mr. Clemens and Mark Twain* (Simon & Schuster, 1966), to more recent studies such as Louis J. Budd's *Our Mark Twain: The Making of His Public Personality* (University of Pennsylvania, 1983) and Everett Emerson's *The Authentic Mark Twain: A Literary Biography of Samuel L. Clemens* (University of Pennsylvania, 1984). A superb detailed study of Twain's youth is Dixon Wecter's *Sam Clemens of Hannibal* (Houghton Mifflin, 1952). Many other scholars have focused on a single aspect or period of Twain's life, such as the Western, the Nevada, the San Francisco years, the Hawaii visit, the lecture tours, his business interests, his regional brand of humor, and so on.

For aid in understanding Twain's place in literature there are innumerable scholarly articles and books. One of the best is Henry Nash Smith's *Mark Twain: The Development of a Writer* (Harvard, 1962). Some are devoted to a single work of Twain's, such as Walter Blair's *Mark Twain and Huck Finn* (University of California, 1960). Others deal with Twain's standing and influence in various countries, from America to Europe and elsewhere. Many books assess Twain's art and language, his major ideas, his political concerns, and the kinds of social, psychological, or intellectual forces that shaped him.

I should note that my own earlier book, *Mark Twain Himself* (Crowell, 1960), is a pictorial biography. The text is largely in Twain's own words, taken not only from his autobiography but from his letters, notebooks, journalism, sketches, travel pieces, and his fiction. Worked into the mosaic are more than 600 pictures—prints, drawings, cartoons, caricatures, paintings, broadsides, posters, and photographs. I have retraversed bits of that ground for the present work.

INDEX